The Globalization of Inequality

The Globalization
of Inequality

François Bourguignon

Translated by Thomas Scott-Railton

Princeton University Press

Princeton and Oxford

CONTENTS

FOREWORD TO THE ENGLISH EDITION

This book was first published in French in 2012 in the collection *La république des idées*, Le Seuil publisher. A requirement of that collection is for books to be accessible to the widest readership and to be short, not exceeding a limited number of characters. This English version sticks to this commitment to concision and non-technicality. As it is published two years later, however, it expands somewhat on the original French version. Some figures have been updated, two tables have been added, several references are made to important books or articles published since publication in France, and the discussion of several timely issues has been slightly lengthened. I thank three anonymous reviewers for helpful suggestions to expand the original French version. Yet, large portions of the text remain unchanged, and I thank Thomas Scott-Railton for rendering it so well in English.

The Globalization of Inequality

INTRODUCTION

Globalization and Inequality

There has been a great deal of debate around the subject of globalization. It has been depicted as a panacea, an instrument for modernization, and a mortal threat. Some believe it has contributed to the "wealth of nations" by making them on the whole more efficient. Others feel it has caused the majority of humanity to sink into poverty in order to benefit a privileged elite. Criticism has been heaped upon it. Globalization is said to be the cause of economic crises, the destruction of the environment, the excessive importance of finance and the financial sector, deindustrialization, the standardization of culture, and many other ills of contemporary society, including an explosive rise in inequality.

My goal is to shed some light on this debate by focusing on one of the above points in particular, one that has arguably drawn the most attention: inequality. Globalization is a complex historical phenomenon that has existed, in some form or another, since the beginning of human society, but which we can track with more precision over recent centuries.[1] No one denies that it exists, and there is little doubt that it will continue. The real question is whether, as it is often claimed, globalization is responsible for an unprecedented rise in inequality in the world over the last two decades. Is the globalization that we see today sounding the death knell for equality? If it continues, will it destroy any hope of social justice?

In order to answer this question, it will be essential to distinguish between inequality in standards of living *between countries* and standards of living *within countries*. Once we've done this, a two-part historical trend emerges. On the one hand, after two centuries of rising steadily, inequality in standard of living *between countries* has started to decline. Twenty years ago, the average standard of living in France or Germany was twenty times higher than in China or India. Today this gap has been cut in half. On the other hand, inequality *within* many countries has increased, often following several decades of stability. In the United States, for example, income inequality has risen to levels that have not been seen in almost a century. From the perspective of social justice, the first trend seems decidedly positive, as long as it is not undermined by the second.

Because we have a tendency to look to our surroundings rather than beyond them, the rise in *national inequality* has in general eclipsed the drop in *global inequality*, even though this drop is undeniable. In the public mind, we are living in an increasingly unequal world, one in which "the rich get richer and the poor get poorer." And as the rise in

[1] See, for example, Patrick Boucheron (dir.), *Le Monde au XVe siècle* (Fayard: Paris, 2009), and Suzanne Berger, *Notre première mondialisation* (Paris: La République des Idées/Seuil, 2003).

national inequality, where it has taken place, seems to coincide with the recent acceleration of globalization, we have a tendency to conclude that the latter was responsible for the former, even if, paradoxically, globalization has *also contributed* to a drop in international inequalities. However, once we have looked at it through both national and international lenses, the relationship between globalization and inequality turns out to be more complex than it first appears.

This is how the title of this book, *The Globalization of Inequality*, should be understood. It has two meanings. On the one hand, it is a reference to questions of global inequality. The importance that is given in international economic debates to effectively re-equilibrating standards of living between countries is the clearest sign of this. But the title also resonates with the feeling that a rise in inequalities affects all of the countries on the planet and is becoming a matter of grave concern.

Of course, these two perspectives are not unrelated. The expansion of international trade, the mobility of capital and labor (notably for the most skilled), and the spread of technological innovation have partially bridged the gap between the wealthiest countries and the developing countries. But, at the same time, they have also contributed to a change in income distribution within these economies. Global economic growth has led to certain lines of production emigrating from developed countries to emerging ones, with the result that the demand for unskilled labor has shrunk in more advanced countries—which has led to a drop in its relative compensation. The international mobility of top skills and the growth of global trade have meant that across the world the high end of the wage distribution falls in line with that of the countries where economic elites are the best compensated, and the income stream from capital is everywhere increasing faster than that from labor. Naturally, other factors influence inequality at both the national and international levels: technological progress, the local capacity for economic growth, specific strategies for development, and even the politics of redistribution through taxes and transfers of wealth. But, in the end, how big a role has globalization played?

The goal of this book is to illuminate the relationship between globalization and inequality by carefully distinguishing between global and national inequality, paying close attention to the causes of the two prevailing trends and examining policies that could potentially bring together equality, greater economic efficiency, and globalization.

In the present day, the question of income inequality has returned to the spotlight for economists, social science researchers, and the political world. During the last few years, rising inequality in certain countries, notably the United States, has been the subject of or inspiration for several major books—among which it would be difficult to overstate the importance of two recent books by Joseph Stiglitz and Thomas Piketty, the success of which is a clear sign of the mounting public interest in the issue of inequality.[2] While few books address global income inequality directly, with the exception of Branko Milanovic's *Worlds Apart*,[3] many have analyzed inequalities in development between

[2] Joseph Stiglitz, *The Price of Inequality: How Today's Divided Society Endangers Our Future* (New York: Norton, 2012); Thomas Piketty, *Capital in the Twenty-First Century* (Cambridge, MA: Harvard University Press, 2013).

[3] Branko Milanovic, *Worlds Apart, Measuring International and Global Inequality* (Princeton, NJ: Princeton University Press, 2005).

countries or regions, which are the principal determinants of inequality at the world level. One of this book's contributions is that it combines the two levels of analysis by closely examining the degree to which inequality *between* countries and *within* countries have become substitutes for each other within the globalization process and the dangers such a state of affairs can cause. The central question is whether the increase in inequality observed in the United States, in some European countries, and in some emerging countries may be considered the consequence of a globalization process, which, at the same time, has drastically reduced income differences between developed and developing countries. Does diminishing inequality among countries fuel rising inequality within nations?

Some people would dismiss the issue of inequality altogether. They would argue that, provided everyone in a society has enough to live on and sees his or her welfare improving over time, why worry about whether progress is faster at the top than at the bottom or the middle? As long as inequality per se has no direct and sizable impact on economic progress, it is an issue that should be left to philosophers. Advocates of such a view would also insist that, despite being more unequal than others, some countries have been able to grow as fast if not faster than other countries— even in times of increasing inequality. Of course, the United States is the archetypical example of such a country.

Others would question the definition of inequality, distinguishing between income and opportunity. They hold that inequality of income does not matter as long as people have more or less the same opportunities to become rich. If everybody has the same chance to become Bill Gates, Warren Buffett, or Lady Gaga, then it does not matter whether

Gates's, Buffett's, or Lady Gaga's annual income is 300 or 3,000 times that of someone working at McDonald's.

These questions will be discussed in some depth later in the book, where it will be shown that excessive inequality has negative effects on economic efficiency and individual welfare. More fundamentally, however, the exclusive appropriation of economic progress by a small elite will, after a time and beyond a specific threshold, necessarily undermine the stability of societies. If, indeed, globalization is perceived as benefiting exclusively those with the top incomes—as in the United States, where the real median income and incomes below it barely changed over the last thirty years—then, at some stage, globalization and the economic model behind it are likely to meet increasing political opposition and be brought to a stop through various types of protectionist and other interventionist measures. The general benefits brought to a country by globalization would then be lost. Occupy Wall Street in the United States or *los indignados* in Spain may have been precursors of such a general movement and if inequality keeps increasing, there is a point at which even a minor economic recession is likely to trigger major social disruptions. Where this tipping point lies is unknown, but there is a definite risk in ignoring such a danger, and both society and the economy would experience severe negative consequences well before that tipping point was reached.

This book is intentionally not limited to the study of national inequality in a small number of countries or a single region of the world. Instead, it examines the role played by various common factors, including globalization, and then looks for those factors that are specific to the evolution of inequality within countries that are essentially quite different.

The book contains five chapters. The recent evolution of global inequality, which is to say, between all of the citizens of the world, is a good starting point in that it combines inequality in standards of living among nations—i.e., the difference between rich and poor countries, with inequality inside nations—i.e., the difference between rich and poor within countries. The fact that its general trends have shifted direction marks a historical turning point. This will be the focus of my first chapter.

The second chapter studies the development of national economic inequalities, and the return, in a number of countries (including many developed countries), of certain dimensions of inequality to levels that had not existed for several decades. What are the causes of this reversal? Should we look for them within the context of globalization, or are they in fact specific to individual nations? These questions will be the main theme of the third chapter.

The last two chapters will be both prospective and prescriptive. The intention is to anticipate certain key trends in the future of the global economy, including demographic factors, and to figure out what their significance might be for the future of inequality. The key will then be to identify economic and social policies that would be best suited to preserving the convergence of standards of living between countries while halting the deterioration of national income distributions. Although on paper it still seems as if it might be possible to redistribute the products of economic activity and prevent inequalities from worsening, we must not forget that any redistribution has potentially significant economic costs and would be subject to political constraints that cannot be ignored.

At the end of this analysis, I will present some conclusions that I offer up to ruling elites, political parties, civil society, and citizens in general about what should be done to create a global economy that would be fair and efficient both nationally and internationally.

I endeavor to examine all of these questions in a concise and nontechnical manner. The issues addressed in this book are of major importance for the understanding of our societies and their future. They are sometimes of some analytical complexity, and it is crucial to make them accessible to a wide audience. I hope this book will contribute to that goal.

CHAPTER 1

Global Inequality

Global inequality is defined as the level of inequality between all inhabitants of the world, thus combining rich and poor people in Latin America as well as in Europe or in the United States. Although this topic has not received much attention, it presents a rather complex combination of inequality *between* nations and inequality *within* nations. This has two major implications. First, global inequality is considerably higher than the inequality we see on average at the national level, given that it combines inequalities among citizens of the same country with disparities in average income between countries. Second, the way that global inequality has evolved over time is in fact the conjunction of two different trends, that of inequality within countries between poor and rich in, for example, France or in Nigeria; and that of inequality between countries, that is to say, between the average person in France and the average person in Nigeria. These trends can sometimes balance each other out and sometimes reinforce each other. Following a brief description of the methods that are used to estimate global inequality, this chapter will examine both its levels and its evolution.

Measuring Global Inequality

The first question that comes up when talking about inequality is: inequality of what? There is inequality of individual earnings, family income, wealth, consumer spending, or individual economic well-being. At the global level, I will be interested in inequalities of "standard of living" between citizens of this planet, defined as household income per member as reported in surveys conducted in most countries using representative samples of households. The numbers that I cite in this chapter and in the tables that follow refer to a constant sample of 106 countries (34 developed countries and 72 developing countries) for which at least two surveys are available over the 1990–2010 period, which allows us to take into account the evolution of inequality within these countries and its contribution to changes in global inequality.[1] On average, these 106 countries, which I list at the end of the chapter, represent a little more than 90% of the world's population.

There are several databases that compile the data obtained from these household surveys. For developing countries, I will use the "Povcal" database, which is run by the World Bank, and for developed countries I will use the

---

[1] The dates that the numbers on distribution in these various countries were available did not always coincide with the years selected for the estimation of global inequality. A certain degree of approximation and interpolation with regard to the original data was therefore necessary.

"OECD Database on Household Income Distribution and Poverty."

In order to make comparisons using this national data, it will need to be adjusted in several ways. The first adjustment comes from the fact that we want to express the standards of living observed at the national level through a metric of equivalent purchasing power. Converting incomes earned in pesos, rupees, or CFA francs into dollars (or euros) according to the official exchange rates is easy. However, since the prices, in dollars, for the same goods differ from one country to another, the numbers this would give us would not be truly comparable in terms of purchasing power; $100 does not buy the same volume of goods in New York that it does in Delhi when converted into rupees. We therefore need to adjust official exchange rates so that the conversion into dollars takes into account differences in the price of the same bundle of goods in various countries. International price comparisons make it possible to fine-tune indicators of "purchasing power parity," which in turn enable us to express standard of living in different countries in dollars and the purchasing power of a dollar in the United States in a given year. This adjustment is smaller for developed countries than for developing countries because prices are relatively similar and not too far from prices in the United States in the former. It may be sizable for developing countries, especially the poorest ones. It is not uncommon to need to multiply the numbers obtained using the official exchange rates by 2.5 or more. Absent any further specification, the numbers I will use for standards of living in this chapter will be expressed in the purchasing power of U.S. dollars from 2005.[2]

[2] To turn these into 2014 U.S. dollars, multiply them by 1.15. New pur-

Another source of incomparability is the way household size is taken into account when estimating the standard of living of an individual. The Povcal data define the standard of living of a person by simply dividing the income (or the consumer spending) of the household to which they belong by the number of household members. The OECD data, on the other hand, refer to income per equivalent adult, each member of the household being given a weight that depends on age and the number of household members. Adjustment is therefore necessary for these two databases to become comparable.[3]

Another, more serious source of heterogeneity within the national data on standards of living we are concerned with is the definition of household "income." In some countries, surveys collect data exclusively on income, in others, on consumer spending. Agricultural income and independent workers' earnings are estimated with varying degrees of imprecision. Income in some surveys includes virtual income, such as the rent implicit in owning one's own house, which is the amount a household could expect to pay if it were to rent its current house at market rates, while others leave these out. Some ignore the role played by

chasing power parities have been released recently based on price statistics collected in 2011 (see http://siteresources.worldbank.org/ICPEXT /Resources/ICP_2011.html). Their release is too recent for the Povcal database to have been revised. As they lead to relative real standards of living somewhat different from the figures based on 2005 prices for some countries, most noticeably China, estimates of the absolute level of global inequality would differ from those reported below, but not its estimated evolution over the last two decades.

[3] In practice, we simply multiplied individual standards of living by the ratio of the aggregate number of equivalent adults/population in OECD countries. It stands to reason that this operation would also modify the distribution itself, but without the possibility of accessing the individual data, correcting for this discrepancy was not possible.

taxes and transfers of income that households pay or receive. And so on. Finally, from the perspective of international comparability, the income or consumer spending of households does not take into account the availability of goods and services that are offered for free by the state and that, to varying degrees depending on the country in question, impact the livelihood of the population.

There are two schools of thought as to how we should address the heterogeneity of our sources across countries. The first recommends that we keep the numbers as is—after having converted them into international purchasing power—thus ignoring the preceding sources of heterogeneity. The second says that we should apply a factor of proportionality to the individual datasets such that the average standard of living is consistent with national accounts, deemed to be more homogeneous than household surveys. Thus, some authors normalize household survey data so that the mean standard of living in a country will be equal to per capita household consumption in the national accounts of that country. In what follows, I will be reporting on household survey means as well as on household survey figures normalized by GDP per capita rather than national accounts' private consumption expenditures per capita. GDP includes the public goods delivered by the state and implicitly consumed for free by households—but also some monetary flows that don't accrue to them—like undistributed firms' profits. It is also the case that, in developing countries, GDP data are more frequently available than aggregate household spending in national accounts.

This choice is not without its critics.[4] On the one hand, it is clear that normalizing the data from household sur-

---

[4] For an in-depth discussion of this issue of using original survey data versus national accounts, see Sudhir Anand and Paul Segal, "What Do We

veys to per capita GDP in order to measure standards of
living is not neutral from the point of view of distribution.
The income missing from the surveys, the taxes, and transfers in cash or in kind that are omitted, the consumption
of public goods, and so forth, are certainly not proportional to reported income in the surveys. What's more, we
know that per capita GDP is a very imperfect indicator of
the economic well-being of a nation's citizens. The Sen-
Stiglitz-Fitoussi[5] report on the need to go "beyond GDP"
to measure social welfare was enough to convince anyone
who might have remained undecided. Unfortunately, we
are still some way from having the statistics we would need
to improve our comparative measures of individual standards of living for a representative sample of countries and
over the long term. For a while longer, international comparisons, such as those that attempt to evaluate global inequality, will have to employ this crude approximation of
well-being. Conversely, we must also recognize that, given
the heterogeneity mentioned above, we should be cau-
tious about estimating the average well-being of a national
population using data on income or consumption taken

Know about Global Income Inequality?" *Journal of Economic Literature* 46,
no. 1 (2008): 57–94; and "The Global Distribution of Income" in Anthony
B. Atkinson and François Bourguignon, *Handbook of Income Distribution*,
volume 2 (Amsterdam: Elsevier, forthcoming). For the GDP per capita approach, see Xavier Sala-i-Martin, "The World Distribution of Income: Falling Poverty and . . . Convergence, Period," *Quarterly Journal of Economics*
121, no. 2 (December 2006): 351–97; and for its critique, see Branko Milanovic, "The Ricardian Vice: Why Sala-i-Martin's Calculations of World Income Inequality Are Wrong" (Washington, DC: World Bank, November
2002).

   [5] Joseph E. Stiglitz, Amartya Sen, and Jean-Paul Fitoussi (with a preface
by Nicolas Sarkozy), *Mismeasuring Our Lives: Why GDP Doesn't Add Up*
(New York: New Press, 2010).

from household surveys. The lively debate sparked in India by the divergence between the growth rate of household consumption expenditure per capita as given by the national accounts and by household surveys in the 1990s is proof that there can be a potentially significant divergence between the two approaches.[6] This divergence is even more problematic when it comes to establishing the comparative framework necessary for estimating global inequality.

But this particular methodological divergence is not necessarily a problem when it comes to tracking the evolution of global inequality over time. We can imagine that the ratio between the estimates obtained using these two methods should not change drastically, or only slowly over a long period of time. Yet, while this appears to be the case in recent history, prudence requires that we examine the numbers obtained through both approaches. Although in this chapter I will give priority to normalizing to capita GDP, the appendix to this chapter shows detailed results obtained with and without this normalization, and shows that indeed the direction of change in global inequality is the same with both approaches.

Another methodological issue concerns which statistical unit to consider. At the national level, it is natural that the unit be the individual, adult or child, active or inactive. Each individual in the population is assigned the income (or the consumption expenditure) of the household to which he or she belongs, divided by the number of its

---

[6] For more on this debate, see Angus Deaton and Valerie Kozel, eds., *The Great Indian Poverty Debate* (Delhi: Macmillan India, 2005); and Angus Deaton, "Measuring Poverty in a Growing World or Measuring Growth in a Poor World," *Review of Economics and Statistics* 87, no. 1 (February 2005): 1–19.

members. Expanding this to the global level consists in simply juxtaposing national populations and looking at the distribution of individual standards of living over a population of 6 or 7 billion people. The high end of this distribution includes wealthy Americans, Europeans, and Saudis, but also includes wealthy Indians and South Africans. Similarly, the low end of the distribution includes a lot of Africans and South Asians, but also the Chinese, Bolivian, Filipino, and Thai poor.

In order to understand the evolution of global inequality over time, it can be useful to isolate the relative roles of inequality between countries and inequality within countries. However, measuring inequality between countries requires that we switch statistical units, shifting over to the country, rather than its nationals, as our unit and assigning it the average standard of living of its inhabitants. This is the definition of global inequality implicitly referenced by the abundant macroeconomic literature of the 1990s on the subject of economic growth and more specifically on the question of whether forces existed that would lead to the "convergence" of per capita national income between countries.[7] In this case, we have to address the question of whether or not we should weight countries by population. Depending on which answer we choose, inequality levels can vary greatly. There is a very high level of inequality between the standards of living of the Chinese and the Luxembourgers. But a fictional population that consisted of 1.3 billion Chinese people and half a million Luxembourgers, with each person assigned the average standard of liv-

[7] See, for example, Charles I. Jones, "On the Evolution of the World Income Distribution," *Journal of Economic Perspectives* 11, no. 3 (Summer 1997): 19–36.

ing of his or her country of origin, would actually be quite equal, given that the rich Luxembourgers would represent only a negligible fraction of the total population.

This question of statistical units to consider leads us to examine different definitions of global standards of living inequality. I will primarily use two definitions: inequality "between countries" (or "international" inequality), which describes the inequality that we would observe in the world if all the nationals of a country had the mean income of that country; and "global" inequality, which, in addition, takes into account intranational disparities in standards of living. An alternative to the between countries inequality is obtained when considering income disparities between representative nationals, in other words giving the same weight to all countries, rather than weighting them by their population (as in the example of China and Luxembourg). When using identical country weights, I use the term "international income scale" and refer to the inequalities on this scale.[8]

The following example illustrates these various concepts. There are two countries A and B with mean income YA in the first country and YB in country B. There are four people, two rich and two poor, in country A, and only two, one rich and one poor, in country B. Finally, poor and rich people have an income YAp and YAr in country A, and YBp and YBr in country B, respectively. With these notations, the three types of distribution just described are as follows:

---

[8] Milanovic (*Worlds Apart*) uses the term inequality "between countries" to describe this and uses "international" inequality when countries are weighted by population. That being said, the "between countries/international" distinction is often ambiguous.

(YAp, YAp,YAr, YAr, YBp, YBr): global distribution and global
   inequality
(YA, YA, YA, YA, YB, YB): international distribution and
   between country inequality
(YA, YB): international income scale

A third question about definitions concerns the measurement of inequality. There are many ways to describe
the statistical distribution of a quantitative variable within
a population, whether it be height, weight, or standard of
living. We might choose to focus only on the extremes of
the distribution: the portion of total income that goes to
the wealthiest or poorest 5%, 10%, or 20%, for example, or
even the average income of the wealthiest X% in comparison to that of the poorest Y%. But we can also try to take
into account the differences observed at intermediate levels. Various synthetic methods of measuring inequality do
this in different ways.

In this book, I will use basically four measures of inequality: the share that goes to the richest (1%, 5%, or
10%), the relative gap between standards of living in the
extreme deciles (the richest 10% and the poorest 10%), the
Gini coefficient, and the Theil coefficient. The Gini coefficient is probably the most frequently employed measure of
inequality. It takes into account the entirety of the distribution rather than just the extremes and can be defined as
(half) the average absolute difference between two individuals chosen at random in the population, in relation to
the average standard of living of the population as a whole.
For example, in a society where the average standard of living is $40,000, a Gini coefficient of 0.4 would mean that
the average gap between two individuals chosen at random

in the population would be \$32,000.[9] The Theil coefficient also takes into account the full range of the distribution. For any decomposition of the population into distinct groups, it has the property that it can be broken down into the sum of inequality *between* groups and the inequality *within* groups, which is clearly an advantage in the present case. In the previous example, the Theil coefficient corresponding to the global distribution can be decomposed into the Theil coefficient corresponding to the between country distribution (YA, YA, YA, YA, YB, YB) and the average of the Theil coefficient of inequality within the countries A and B, which depends only on the differences YAr-YAp and YBr-YBp.

A final question about definitions must be addressed: the difference between inequality and poverty. One could criticize the measurements just given for being relative. That the poorest 10% have a standard of living ten times lower than the richest 10% does not mean the same thing in India that it does in Luxembourg. In India, it means that the poorest 10% have difficulty surviving or are one economic incident away from starvation, which is not the case in Luxembourg. It is therefore important to introduce an absolute norm into the evaluation of global inequality. An easy way of doing this is to define an absolute threshold of poverty and count the number of persons who fall below it. The most commonly used threshold is "1.25 dollars per person per day" in 2005 international purchasing power. This number corresponds to the official poverty threshold that is used by the poorest countries in the world that have

[9] This coefficient has a range between zero, perfect equality, and one, total inequality, which is to say, a situation in which one individual would receive all national income.

established such a threshold. It is often called "extreme poverty." A higher, less exclusive, threshold of 2.50 dollars per person per day is also widely used.

Global Inequality at the End of the 2000s

No matter how you measure it, global inequality is considerable, probably above the level of what a national community could bear without risking a major crisis. It is in any event considerably higher than the levels of inequality generally observed at the national level, as we can see by using a few countries as examples.

In the year 2008—which I will use as my reference point, because it was the last year before the global economic crisis from which the world has yet to fully recover—the per capita GDP in France was around $33,000 (in 2005 international purchasing power), but the average disposable income per person, or the individual standard of living, as recorded in the household surveys, was only $20,500.[10] The richest 10% received 24.5% of total income and almost seven times as much income as the poorest 10%. Their standard of living was approximately $45,000 per capita per year, more than twice the national average, while that of the bottom 10% was only $6,600. France's Gini coefficient, as defined earlier, was 0.29. This means that on average, the gap between the standard of living of two people

---

[10] This difference is due to corporate and state income that is not distributed, as well as the differences in how income is defined in household surveys and the national accounts (see above). In what follows, standard of living will generally refer to the mean income per capita given by household surveys.

taken at random was 58% of average income, thus slightly less than $12,000.

Among wealthy countries, France has moderate levels of inequality. The ratio of the standard of living of the richest 10% to the poorest 10% was lower (slightly less than 5, to be precise) in the Scandinavian countries, which have the highest levels of equality among wealthy countries. This ratio was slightly greater than 7 in Germany and the United Kingdom. In Southern Europe, it was close to 10. It was 15 in the United States, the developed country with the highest inequality. In the United States, GDP per capita was $43,000 in 2008, the average standard of living as recorded by the Current Population Survey was around $25,000 per person, that of the richest 10% was $70,000, while that of the poorest 10% was $4,500. The Gini coefficient for the United States was 0.39.

Brazil is an emerging country and also one of the most unequal countries in the world. At $10,000 per person per year (in 2005 international purchasing power), the GDP per capita was higher than in the majority of developing countries, but in 2008 it was still less than one-third of the average European standard of living. The standard of living of the richest 10% was then around $20,000 per person per year, or close to the French average, but the standard of living of the poorest 10% was approximately $350, or close to one-twentieth that of the poorest French. As a result, the gap between the richest 10% and the poorest 10% was higher than 50, and the Gini coefficient was 0.58.

Ethiopia is a poor country in Africa. GDP per capita in 2008 was only $850, whereas the standard of living recorded in the household survey was $660, a sixth of the standard of living of the poorest 10% in France. Inequality is less pronounced than in Brazil, but the disposable income of the poorest 10% is well below the absolute poverty threshold of $1.25 per person per day. In fact, it is equivalent to almost two-thirds of this sum, or $300 per person per year (in international purchasing power). It is hard to imagine how one could survive on such a sum. While the richest Ethiopians are obviously better off, they remain, on average, very poor by European standards. The richest 10% of Ethiopians live on an average of $2,000 per person per year, still very much below the standard of living of the poorest 10% of the French population. Of course, some Ethiopians are better off than the poorest French (or perhaps even than the average French person), but they make up only a handful!

Now let us turn to global inequality. One can guess, from what I've written so far, that it will be considerable: the poorest inhabitants of the world are comparable to the Ethiopian poor, while the richest inhabitants of the world are comparable to the American rich. The gap between the standard of living of the richest 10% of the world and the poorest 10% was above 90 in 2008![11] In absolute values, the poorest 600 million in the world have an average of $270 in disposable income per year, while the richest 600 million have a standard of living above $25,000. Let us remember that in Brazil, one of the most unequal countries in the world, the ratio between the extreme deciles was "only" 50:1! Even if we expand the extreme percentiles that we examine, global inequality remains considerable; the richest 20% have a standard of living that is still forty times higher than the poorest 20%. As for the global Gini coefficient, it was 0.70 for standard of living in 2008 when using household surveys and 0.64 when normalizing to per cap-

[11] For detailed numbers, see the appendix to this chapter.

ita GDP (see appendix). In both cases, it is above the highest levels of inequality seen at the national level in countries like Brazil, or even those that existed in apartheid South Africa.

These numbers thus show a world that is extraordinarily unequal with regard to any national norm. It is easy to see why this would be the case. To the inequality within a country, whether high or low, the global perspective adds the inequality between countries, which in itself is considerable. What I earlier referred to as the "international income scale" shows this. In 2008, the average GDP per person in the twenty richest countries in the world was $40,000 (in purchasing power of 2005 dollars). It was $1,000 in the twenty poorest countries, a ratio of 40:1.

These numbers describe inequality in relative terms, although I have attempted to indicate the absolute standards of living that they imply. But we can also work in absolute terms and say that it is not so much the relationship between the poor and the rich that is important, but the extent of poverty itself, which is to say the total number of persons whose standards of living fall below the threshold of $1.25 per person per day as defined earlier.

According to the World Bank, the number of persons living on less than $1.25 a day, the "threshold of extreme poverty," was 1.3 billion in 2008, which equals approximately 20% of the world population. It was this number that led British economist Paul Collier to title his best-selling book *The Bottom Billion*.[12] With a less extreme definition of poverty, $2.5 per day, the number is even more

[12] Paul Collier, *The Bottom Billion: Why the Poorest Countries Are Failing and What Can Be Done About It* (Oxford: Oxford University Press, 2007).

overwhelming. Using this metric, our world has 3 billion people in poverty—almost half of humanity!

These measurements can be criticized for being based on an absolute definition of poverty, given that there is also a relative side to poverty (the comparisons that individuals make with each other). This is why the European Union defines the poverty threshold for its member states relatively, in relationship to the median standard of living of the country in question (the standard of living that divides the population into two groups of equal size). Using this type of definition, poverty is no longer exclusive to poor countries, as it is actually representative of inequality in the standard of living distribution. But applying this concept to the world population and lumping together under the title "poverty" Bolivian households whose purchasing power is only $100 per person per year with American households that live with $5,000 in disposable income seems senseless. In one case it is survival itself that is at stake; in others, it is social status and dignity.

Examining inequality at the global level reveals a world that appears profoundly unjust from the perspective of the implicit criteria of social justice frequently invoked in national politics. Economic inequality has reached a level far above what exists today within most national communities. Is it possible to imagine that a tenth of a nation's population could enjoy a standard of living ninety times higher than another tenth? What's more, this inequality condemns nearly half of humanity to poverty and has made survival itself precarious for more than a fifth of humanity.

Of course, there are other dimensions to inequality and poverty than income: access to basic infrastructure, health, education, access to the legal system, or ability to participate in public decision-making, among others. We could have covered them in more detail, even though they are often harder to observe on an individual basis.[13] Across countries, on the other hand, they turn out to be highly, but not perfectly, correlated with differences in income per capita.

This is the sad snapshot of world inequality today. Any snapshot, however, is marked by the moment in which it was taken. The global distribution of standard of living is certainly dramatically unequal, but has this always been the case? Are things on track to improve or, on the contrary, are they getting worse?

A Historic Turning Point

Opinion is divided on the subject of the evolution of global standard of living inequality. One often hears that "global inequality keeps getting worse and worse." The 2005 Human Development Report made this argument and it has since been echoed from various corners.[14] But one also hears that the impressive development in China, and in emerging countries in general, has led to a dramatic reduction in inequality and poverty in the world. So what is actually the case?

If we use the definition of global inequality (between the standards of living of individuals in the global population as a whole), there is little doubt as to its trajectory. After having risen steadily since the beginning of the nine-

---

[13] See, for example, Esther Duflo, *Le Développement humain : lutter contre la pauvreté (I)* (Paris: La République des idées/Seuil, 2010).

[14] "International Cooperation at a Crossroads: Aid, Trade and Security in an Unequal World," *Human Development Report 2005* (New York: UNDP, 2005).

teenth century, it has now begun to fall rapidly, mostly due to the performance of emerging countries. This reversal began two decades ago—when normalizing the standard of living to GDP per capita—but has accelerated since the start of the new millennium. The reversal took place somewhat later, when standards of living were left uncorrected; see table 2 in the appendix to this chapter.

Figure 1 shows the evolution of various measures of global inequality from the beginning of the nineteenth century to the present day. The data come, on the one hand, from an approximate estimation of historical data made several years ago, and on the other, from more precise estimates for the more recent period (1990–2008) based on statistics on the standard of living distribution in the sample of countries described earlier. In both cases, the national standard of living numbers have been normalized to per capita GDP.

This graph shows two important things. The first is the explosion in global inequality that took place over the course of the nineteenth century and the majority of the twentieth century. The Industrial Revolution in the early nineteenth century marks the point where the large economies of Western Europe "took off" and accrued disparities appeared at the global level that had previously existed first and foremost at the national level. This rise continued up until the final quarter of the twentieth century, with the exception of a slight equalization following the end of World War II, principally as a result of the implementation of redistributive policies in several countries (to which we should add the effects of the Chinese Revolution and the integration of Central and Eastern Europe into the Soviet bloc). This rise is quite impressive. In 1820, the richest 10% in the world enjoyed a standard of living twenty times

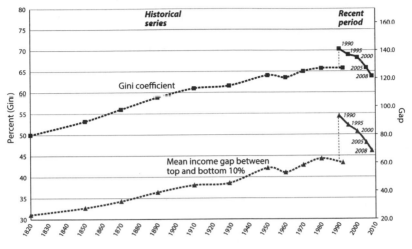

Figure 1. Evolution of World Inequality, 1820–2008.

Sources: The historical data come from François Bourguignon and Christian Morrisson, "Inequality Among World Citizens: 1820–1992," *American Economic Review* 92, no. 4 (2002): 727–44. It uses estimates of GDP per person provided by Angus Maddison (in *Monitoring the World Economy*, Paris: OECD Development Centre, 1995). The recent data represent an update of the article by François Bourguignon, "A Turning Point in Global Inequality . . . and Beyond," in *Research on Responsibility. Reflections on Our Common Future*, ed. Wilhem Krull (Leipzig: CEP Europaische Verlagsanstalp, 2011). The indexes of purchasing power parity that Angus Maddison used for the historical data referenced the year 1990. The data for the recent period use purchasing power parity data based on price statistics that were collected in 2005, which sometimes resulted in significant revisions to the parity indexes. This explains much of the discontinuity between the two series in 1990.

higher than the poorest 10%; by 1980, this number would be three times larger. The Gini coefficient in 1820 was around 0.5, similar to a relatively unequal country today. By 1980 it was 0.66, higher than any existing level of national inequality.

The second striking point that this graph shows is a sharp decline beginning in 1990 (the "recent period" in figure 1). Changes in datasets and purchasing power parity measurements resulted in a change in the estimation of global inequality—hence the discontinuity in the series shown in figure 1. Nonetheless, in relation to the historical series, the drop in inequality is both undeniable and sizable. In the last twenty years, the Gini coefficient and even the relative gap between the two extreme deciles decreased almost as much as they had increased since 1900. The turn of the millennium therefore marks a watershed moment in the evolution of global inequality.[15]

There has also been a parallel reversal in terms of absolute poverty. Economic growth has led to a steady drop in the proportion of people in situations of poverty in the world. Insofar as the poverty thresholds used today would have been meaningful a century ago (keeping purchasing power constant), we could estimate that extreme poverty (less than $1.25 per person per day in 2005 American prices) affected more than 70% of the global population at the beginning of the twentieth century. We saw that this proportion is now below 20%. Because of population growth, however, the decrease in the percentage of people in poverty has not been accompanied by a drop in the absolute number of people in poverty. Therefore, approximately 1.2 billion people were in extreme poverty in 1929, and the number today is similar, even slightly higher.

What occurred between these two dates is of considerable importance. Despite a more or less continuous drop in the proportion of poor people in the world, their absolute

[15] Christian Morrisson and Fabrice Murtin ("Inégalité interne des revenus et inégalité mondiale," document de travail P26, FERDI, 2011) have extended the historical data to cover the recent period without any methodological adjustments. They found much the same evolution over the last twenty years.

number kept going up because of global population growth. There were approximately 2 billion people living in extreme poverty in the early 1980s; however, the last twenty years have witnessed a considerable decline in that number. Since 1990, the number of people in poverty has dropped by around 500 million individuals. For the first time since the Industrial Revolution two centuries ago, economic progress is moving more quickly than population growth, in part because the latter has slowed down but overwhelmingly because of accelerated growth in average income per capita in the developing world. This is a stunning turn of events.

Given these undeniable statistics, why do we still read and hear that global inequality continues to worsen? The answer to this question has two parts. The first is purely statistical. As we have seen, the numbers for the recent period in figure 1 refer to the standard of living distribution after normalization to a particular country's GDP per person. In fact, once we stop normalizing and use the original household survey data, estimates of global distribution show a slightly slower reversal in inequality trends. The acceleration then takes place in the 2000s rather than the mid-1990s.[16] Since this represents a more recent phenomenon, maybe it has not registered for everyone yet.

[16] See table 2 in the appendix to this chapter. Using a different database, Christoph Lakner and Branko Milanovic ("Global Income Distribution: From the Fall of the Berlin Wall to the Great Recession," World Bank Policy Research Working Paper No. 6719, Washington, DC, 2013) found the same drop in inequality in the 2000s, although less pronounced than in table 2. Two recent draft papers reach the same conclusion. The first one, by Miguel Niño-Zarazay, Laurence Roopez, and Finn Tarp, "Global Interpersonal Inequality: Trends and Measurement" (WIDER Working Paper 2014/004) based on GDP per capita normalized data finds that the drop in global inequality may have started around 1980. The second one, by Rahul

A second explanation for the apparent lack of consensus about the evolution of global inequality is conceptual. There are in fact several ways of defining global inequality. Should we take into account inequality within countries, as we did previously, or look only at a country's average income and, if so, should we weight it by population or not? It turns out that global inequality evolves differently based on which definition one uses. Paradoxically, while global inequality, as we have considered it so far, has diminished since the 1990s, disparities between the extremes of the international income scale, using per person GDP, continue to increase. Without weighting for population, the fifteen richest countries in the dataset used for the recent period in figure 1 had an average GDP per person thirty-eight times higher than that of the fifteen poorest countries in 1990. This number had risen to forty-four by 2008.

The exceptional growth in Asian countries and the relatively weak performance of many African countries in the course of the last twenty years can explain this apparent contradiction. Once countries are weighted by population, the rapid growth of per inhabitant GDP in China (8% per year), India (4% per year), and several other Asian countries (Indonesia, Bangladesh, Vietnam); compared with the growth in richer countries (2% per year), explains the decline in the relative gap and in inequality between the populations of rich countries and the populations of poor countries in general. At the same time, the weak growth in per capita income in many African countries, some of

---

Lahoti, Arjun Jayadev, and Sanjay G. Reddy, "The Global Consumption and Income Project (GCIP): An Introduction and Preliminary Findings" (available at SSRN:http://ssrn.com/abstract=2480636), based on household survey means, also finds a drop in global inequality since the mid-1980s, with a clear acceleration in the 2000s.

which even experienced negative growth over the last twenty years, explains the divergence between the richest and the poorest countries when we do not take size into account. In fact, what is remarkable is that the composition of the latter group has changed significantly over time. Among the fifteen poorest countries, several countries, almost all of them Asian, have left this group in the last few decades and it is now composed mostly of African countries, several of which experienced severe recessions brought on by internal conflicts that temporarily paralyzed their economies or even caused them to move backward (e.g., Burundi, Central African Republic, Madagascar, Sierra Leone, and others).

How should we think about this? Which definition should we keep? In fact, both of them are important. If we wish to adopt a global perspective and look at the population of the world as a whole, we cannot leave out the demographic weights of various countries, and it is the drop in global inequality in figure 1 to which we should give preference. We could then say that, after two centuries of steady economic growth, global inequality has significantly decreased over the last twenty years. But this should not mask the fact that a small number of less populous countries have fallen significantly behind the rest of the world. In other words, certain poor countries have only marginally benefited from the global rise in prosperity and have fallen even further behind the top end, and even the median, of the distribution. The decrease in global inequality should not distract us from this worrisome situation. For those who think about global welfare in terms of the standard of living of the very poorest people and countries in the world, there was no improvement over the last two decades. A related fact is that the recent drop in global inequality is less pronounced and occurs later when big Asian countries are left out of inequality measurement.

Another negative feature of this development is the increase in the gap between absolute standards of living that we continue to observe in the world, despite the drop in relative inequality. Even if the standard of living in rich countries is growing more slowly than in a good number of developing countries, a particular level of growth in a rich country represents a far larger increase in absolute standard of living than the same rate of growth would in a developing country. Therefore, fairly rapid growth in these countries will not necessarily bridge the absolute gap; while the relative gap between the richest 10% and the poorest 10% in the world has shrunk from above ninety in 1990 to below seventy in 2008, the absolute difference in standard of living between these two populations has grown by about $10,000, and today stands at around $50,000. Some observers are more sensitive to this aspect of inequality than to relative gaps between rich and poor.[17]

To summarize, if we wish to stick with relative definitions of inequality, our conclusions about world poverty and inequality in the 2000s will have to be nuanced. It is undeniable that the situation is dramatic and that standard of living inequality is considerable. And it is undeniable that extreme poverty affects almost one-sixth of humanity. But this situation has also undergone a spectacular improvement throughout the last two decades, thanks to rapid growth in several developing countries, notably the most populous ones.

[17] An early discussion of this point can be found in Serge-Christophe Kolm, "Unequal Inequalities I," *Journal of Economic Theory* 12 (1976): 416–42.

The Great Gap

Some measures of inequality, different from the ones used previously, allow us to subdivide total inequality among the inhabitants of the world. As previously explained, one may distinguish that part of global inequality due to differences in standards of living *between* countries on the one hand, and on the other, that part due to the average inequality *within* countries. When applied to the historical period, this distinction shows the very decisive role played by differences between countries in the explosion of global inequality since the beginning of the nineteenth century. These inter-country differences were themselves reflections of profound divergences between processes of economic growth. At the same time, average inequality within countries dropped significantly, especially around the middle of the twentieth century. Starting in the 1990s, however, we can see these two trends begin to go into reverse so that inequality between countries begins to decrease significantly, while average inequality within countries has begun to grow slightly, after a long period during which it had remained stable.[18]

The evolution of inequality between countries essentially reflects the logic of the growth of the global economy and the way it spread geographically. Starting in the beginning of the twentieth century, the Industrial Revolution led to rapid growth in the Western European countries, then in their ex-colonies in the New World, starting with the United States. For more than a century and a half, global economic growth was located almost exclusively in

[18] See table 1 in the appendix to this chapter.

these countries, which on average represented a little less than one-fifth of the world's population in this period.

This gap in growth tends to shrink after World War II and the rise in inter-country inequality slows, then stops. While Japan first saw significant growth during the inter-war period, the Asian "dragons" (South Korea, Hong Kong, Singapore, Taiwan) began to experience strong growth after the war, and the Latin American countries saw accelerated growth during the Second World War as a result of strong policies of import substitution. Growth also accelerated in the European colonies that achieved independence.

Finally, the gap between rates of growth in developed countries and developing countries would reverse slightly before the turn of the twenty-first century. For more than two decades now, developing countries have been catching up. This began in Asian countries, notably the Indian and Chinese giants, marching in the steps of the Asian dragons, and since then has spread progressively to a large portion of the developing world, including the African continent in the 2000s.

The determinants of economic growth are numerous and often vary according to the characteristics of the country in question. But there is a large body of empirical literature that suggests there are also a number of common factors that play a significant role. The most important of these are, on the one hand, organizational and technological innovations, and, on the other hand, the accumulation of factors of production, whether material factors such as production equipment and infrastructure or non-material factors such as education, job training, and scientific or technical know-how. These two groups of factors do a great deal to explain the development gap that accumulated between today's developed countries and other parts of the world since the beginning of the Industrial Revolution, as well as the growth differential in favor of emerging countries that we see today. As far as the latter is concerned, the existing development gap means that innovation itself is less of a constraining factor, to the extent that developing countries can observe the experiences of developed countries and imitate them. Once the political and social climates allow for these factors to accumulate rapidly, growth can take off without any major constraints. One could say that developed countries are on the "frontier" of technology and must grow along with it, while developing countries are still some way from this frontier. Therefore, their ability to grow will depend mostly on their capacity to accumulate factors of production as well as to adapt technological and organizational standards observed in developed countries to their particular situations.[19]

In accordance with this mechanism, we could say that the developing world has begun a steady process of catchup with the rich countries. Globalization partially explains this reversal. The access to the technology and to the markets of the Northern countries has certainly played an important role in the accelerated growth of the developing countries in the global South. Moreover, the rapid increase in the volume of South-South exchange is starting to create a greater degree of autonomy for the developing world. Now that the virtues of accumulation have been demonstrated through the examples of a few large emerging countries, it would be surprising if, barring any natural catastro-

[19] See, for example, Daron Acemoglu, Philippe Aghion, and Fabrizio Zilibotti, "Distance to Frontier, Selection, and Economic Growth," *Journal of the European Economic Association* 4, no. 1 (2006): 37–74.

phes or massive political reversals, growth in this part of the world slowed in a lasting manner.

Of course, this does not mean that all developing countries will experience sustained growth. The factors that allow for accumulation to occur are not present together everywhere and at all times. There will continue to be countries that lag behind in cases where weak social or political institutions prevent efficient accumulation or when tensions and conflicts temporarily reverse the processes of growth. In a general sense, however, it would seem that the extended rise in inequality between countries that defined the nineteenth century and a good portion of the twentieth century is over. After a short period during which it remained on a plateau, an enduring decrease began. The "great gap" in standards of living between developed countries and emerging countries is beginning to close—albeit slowly—thanks to a "great gap" in growth rates pushing in the opposite direction. Over the last two decades, the income differential between developed and developing countries has fallen by a little more than 20%, whereas the growth rate differential has moved from zero to close to 3% in favor of the latter.

An important point to emphasize about the evolution of between country inequality is the major contribution of China to its evolution. Most of the drop in inequality that took place in the 1990s is due to China's outstanding growth performance. The dismal performance of sub-Saharan Africa and Latin America in the same period would have led to slightly increased global inequality without China. In the following decade, however, the growth gap relative to developed countries extended to the major part of the developing world.

A Reversal of Inequality
within Countries?

What about the other component of global inequality, the average inequality within countries?

Initially high, inequality within countries increased slightly over the course of the nineteenth century. It then declined very markedly between the end of World War I and the post–World War II period, up until the early 1950s. The creation of powerful systems of redistribution (ranging from progressive income taxes to unemployment and other cash benefits, social security, and public health-care) led to an impressive reduction in inequality in the majority of developed countries. But the drop in within country inequality was also due in part to the forced egalitarianism the Russian and Chinese revolutions imposed on the areas they controlled, as well as the creation of the Soviet bloc in 1945.

After this drop, average inequality within countries lingered at more or less constant levels until the start of the 1990s. From the 1990s onward, within country inequality began to climb again slowly but steadily. In terms of contribution to total global inequality, we are still well below the average level observed on the eve of the First World War, but the inversion of the trend seems clear.

How can we evaluate the size of this phenomenon? The decomposition of the Theil coefficient shown in table 1 in the appendix to this chapter suggests an increase in the within component of global inequality as measured by the Theil coefficient around 10%, most of that increase taking place in the last decade. It must be realized, however, that this figure corresponds to some average increase in the degree of inequality within single countries. As we shall see in the next chapter, inequality has very substantially increased in some countries, whereas it has declined in others. What is apparent at the global level is that the overall balance of this effect is positive.

It may thus be the case that the evolution of global inequality is taking a radical turn. The fact that emerging countries and, to a lesser extent, developing countries, are developing more quickly has contributed to the decrease in inequality for the world population as a whole. However, the rise in inequality within nations has tended to increase it. Today, the first trend is much stronger than the second and total inequality is on the decline. It is not unreasonable to worry that this current trend has its limits and that the rise in inequality within countries, or at least in a significant subset of countries, could progressively weaken the fall in global inequality. Over the last decade, roughly 20% of the drop in inequality between countries has been compensated for by an increase in within country inequality. A process of "internalizing" global inequality within national communities may thus take place; inequality between Americans and Chinese would be partly replaced by more inequality between the rich and the poor in America and China. I will return to this not implausible but worrisome scenario later in the book.

The Effects of the Crisis

Given the shocks that the global economy recently endured, and from which it has yet to fully recover, it is interesting to wonder about the effects of the financial crisis that started in 2008 on global inequality. The statistics necessary to extend our comparative international analysis of global inequality much beyond 2008 are not yet fully available. An estimate of the global distribution in 2010 is given in the tables shown in the appendix to this chapter. Also, the split of global inequality into inequality "between countries" and "inequality within countries" will give us a quick idea of recent trends.

The crisis did not slow the process of developing countries catching up with rich countries and, as a result, inequality between countries has continued to decline. The crisis had a more or less uniform negative impact on growth rates across the world so that developing countries retained their advantage over developed countries. They lost a few percentage points of GDP growth, but, overall, their growth rate remained quite positive, whereas growth disappeared or even became negative in the majority of developed countries. Without any change in national inequalities, the Gini coefficient would thus have kept going down since 2008. Of course, it remains to be seen whether slower GDP growth has been accompanied by a worsening of income distribution within countries. Available data suggest that this was not the case as of 2010. This conclusion remains valid once we take into account the fact that individual standards of living seem to have been less affected by the crisis than has the volume of aggregate activity, as represented by the GDP, notably in the developed countries equipped with social safety nets, which include programs such as unemployment insurance and various mechanisms for social assistance. Even so, it is true that standards of living have, on average, continued to rise more quickly in emerging countries, which also recovered much faster from the crisis.

At the beginning of the crisis, there was a lot of talk about the possibility that there might be a "decoupling" of the cycles of developed economies and emerging economies, in the hope that the economic vitality of the latter would make up for the sluggishness of the former. The globalization of trade and the growing interdependency of national economies render such an idea implausible. The decoupling that did in fact take place was structural rather than cyclical. It concerned *trends* in growth; developing economies are on a path to faster long-term growth than are developed economies. The crisis did not change this basic fact about the contemporary global economy.

Detailed Evidence on the Recent Changes in Global Inequality

This appendix provides additional details on the evolution of global income inequality since 1990. It also provides estimates of the evolution of the global distribution during the heavy crisis years, that is, from 2008 to 2010. More recent data on income distribution were not available at the time of writing.

Table 1 contains the inequality numbers from figure 1 over the recent period, as well as some other indicators. It thus refers to standard of living after normalization to GDP per person. The first section concerns the representativeness of the sample of 106 countries used in these estimates. We can see that, on average, this sample represents around 92% of the world population, but also that this share is very slowly declining over time. We can also observe that the countries omitted are countries that are

Table 1. World Income Distribution Indicators, 1990–2008[a] (Household survey data rescaled by GDP per capita)

Year	1990	1995	2000	2005	2008	2010
Mean income per capita in sample In PPP 2005 USD	6950	7210	8070	9025	9890	10070
Share of global population accounted for (%)	92.3	92.2	92.2	92.1	92.0	92.0
Share of global income accounted for (%)	94.3	94.4	94.3	94.0	93.8	93.7
Global inequality						
Gini	0.703	0.690	0.683	0.658	0.638	0.623
Theil	0.949	0.918	0.903	0.827	0.763	0.723
Mean income gap between richest and poorest 10%	93.1	86.7	82.1	74.3	68.5	63.5
Inequality between countries (Theil)	0.734	0.696	0.681	0.600	0.529	0.479
Inequality within countries (Theil)	0.215	0.222	0.222	0.227	0.234	0.244

[a] Inequality computed on income (or consumption expenditure) per capita in PPP 2005 USD after rescaling by national GDP per capita; Povcal and OECD secondary sources used. Constant sample of 106 countries.

slightly poorer than the global average, because the share of the 106 countries in the sample in world GDP is a little larger than their share in the whole population. This second bias is approximately constant since the two move in parallel over time. But the most interesting information in the table, besides the evolution of the overall inequality measures, concerns the decomposition of the Theil coefficient of inequality into a component that describes only the inequality that exists *between* countries (what we would see if every citizen in a country had the same income) and a component that shows the average inequality that exists *within* countries (the inequality that we would see in the world if the average incomes of countries were all equalized). These numbers show us that the decline in inequality over the last twenty years is almost exclusively a result of the decline in inequality between countries, with the average inequality within countries remaining more or less constant until the turn of the millennium but increasing afterward, as emphasized in the text.

Table 2 refers to the estimates obtained with the household survey data, as compiled by the World Bank (Povcal) and the OECD—i.e., without scaling up by GDP per capita. One immediately notices that the average standard of living of the surveyed population as a whole is significantly lower than the average GDP per person in table 1, and that this ratio decreases continually and significantly over the time period being studied. This suggests either that the average coverage rate of these surveys is shrinking with time, or that the share of disposable household income in national income has, on average, decreased considerably. To the extent that it is unlikely that one and/or the other of these phenomena are general across the diverse countries being studied, normalizing to GDP per inhabitant, as done in table 1, may give a more accurate picture of the evolution of global inequality. In a certain sense, this ensures that each country is weighted at all points of time in relation to its economic activity. On the other hand, if the relative decline in income surveyed relative to national accounts can be explained by a decrease in coverage, it is important to emphasize that it is quite unlikely that this change would have been neutral with respect to distribu-

Table 2. World Income Distribution Indicators Based on Household Surveys, 1990–2008[a]

Year	1990	1995	2000	2005	2008	2010
Mean income						
In PPP 2005 USD	3880	3815	4020	4490	4745	4825
As a percentage of mean GDP per capita	55.8	52.9	49.8	49.8	48.0	47.9
Global inequality						
Gini	0.741	0.738	0.734	0.712	0.699	0.691
Mean income gap between richest and poorest 10%	113.2	111.3	102.6	97.5	93.9	90.7
Poverty head count (%)						
Extreme poverty: 1.25 PPP 2005 USD per day	32.4	30.0	24.8	17.6	15.6	15.5
Poverty: 2.5 PPP 2005 USD per day	57.4	54.6	52.1	43.8	40.6	38.6

[a] Inequality computed on income (or consumption expenditure) per capita in PPP 2005 USD; Povcal and OECD secondary sources used. Constant sample of 108 countries.

tion. In fact, it is high-end incomes that tend to be under-represented in these surveys.[1] If this is in fact the case, and to the extent that this bias is more marked for developing economies, then the data from these surveys would tend to overestimate inequality between countries and underestimate inequality within countries.

Not normalizing for GDP per capita greatly increases the degree of inequality in the global standard of living distribution. The reason for this is not, as one might expect,

[1] See, for example, Anton Korinek, Johan A. Mistiaen, and Martin Ravallion, "Survey Nonresponse and the Distribution of Income," *Journal of Economic Inequality* 4 (2006): 33–55.

that the incomes surveyed represent a systematically larger share of GDP in rich countries than in poor countries, but rather that the variance in this ratio is substantially higher in poor countries. Failing to rescale to GDP per capita statistically penalizes a good number of poor countries, making them appear even poorer in relation to the global average, which also contributes to a rise in the reported level of inequality.

What is reassuring is that the evolutions in inequality in table 2 run relatively parallel to those in table 1, albeit at a higher level. In particular, in table 2 the drop in the 1990s is relatively slow—significantly slower than in table 1— and then accelerates quickly during the 2000s. Such a pattern is consistent with the view that disposable household income per person, as given by household survey means, and GDP per capita in national accounts, most likely should follow roughly parallel paths in the long run. The conclusion that the turn of the millennium represented a turning point in the evolution of inequality therefore seems to hold up.

To conclude this technical annex, I will emphasize that these procedures of estimating global standard of living inequality are approximate, not only because household surveys are imprecise, whether in their coverage or in the definition of income that they employ, but also because the national accounts do not necessarily provide an aggregate basis for unambiguous comparisons between countries. Sensitivity analysis does show, however, that from a dynamic perspective, the problem of imprecise data for distribution within countries is probably a secondary concern. As we saw in table 1, the variations in global inequality are above all the result of variations in inequality between countries.

Countries Included in the Estimation of the Global Distribution
of Living Standard

Argentina	Iceland	Philippines
Australia	India	Poland
Austria	Indonesia	Portugal
Bangladesh	Iran, Islamic Rep.	Romania
Belgium	Ireland	Russian Federation
Bolivia	Israel	Rwanda
Brazil	Italy	Senegal
Burkina Faso	Jamaica	Sierra Leone
Burundi	Japan	Slovak Republic
Cameroon	Jordan	Slovenia
Canada	Kazakhstan	South Africa
Central African	Kenya	Spain
Republic	Korea, Rep.	Sri Lanka
Chile	Kyrgyz Republic	Sudan
China	Lao PDR	Suriname
Colombia	Latvia	Swaziland
Costa Rica	Luxembourg	Sweden
Cote d'Ivoire	Macedonia, FYR	Switzerland
Czech Republic	Madagascar	Syrian Arab Republic
Denmark	Malaysia	Tajikistan
Dominican Republic	Mali	Tanzania
Ecuador	Mauritania	Thailand
Egypt, Arab Rep.	Mexico	Togo
El Salvador	Morocco	Trinidad and Tobago
Estonia	Mozambique	Tunisia
Ethiopia	Nepal	Turkey
Finland	Netherlands	Uganda
France	New Zealand	Ukraine
Georgia	Nicaragua	United Kingdom
Germany	Niger	United States
Ghana	Nigeria	Uruguay
Greece	Norway	Venezuela, RB
Guatemala	Pakistan	Vietnam
Guinea	Panama	Yemen, Rep.
Honduras	Paraguay	
Hungary	Peru	

CHAPTER 2

Are Countries Becoming More Unequal?

After a significant decline in the mid-twentieth century, followed by a long period of stability, inequality has begun to rise over the last two or three decades in the large majority of developed countries. It has also risen in a number of developing countries for which we have long-term data. This phenomenon is therefore not isolated to a few cases, such as the oft-cited examples of the United States and China. Are there deep trends underlying these developments? As suggested in the preceding chapter, is inequality between countries in the world on the verge of being supplanted by inequality within countries?

This chapter analyzes the evolution of inequality in developed and developing countries. It first focuses on several dimensions of income and wealth inequality and then moves to non-monetary aspects of economic inequality which, at the national level, may be equally important in the public perception of changes in the social fairness or unfairness of the economy they live in.

The Rise in National Income Inequality

It would be difficult to begin a discussion of national inequality with any country other than the United States, given how spectacular the rise in inequalities has been in that country. Figure 2, which extends Thomas Piketty and Emmanuel Saez's estimates, illustrates this quite well.[1] By 2008, just before the recent crisis, the level of income inequality, as measured by the share of the top 10% tax units in total household market income, had returned to levels that had not been seen in a century. The Gini coefficient of gross income per person shows a similar evolution. After forty years of stable inequality, American society seems to be purely and simply erasing the drop in inequality that took place in the wake of the Great Depression and World War II. Moreover, the crisis does not seem to have reversed this steadily increasing trend toward greater inequality.

This graph uses primary income data, which is income from activity prior to taxes and transfers to households. Once we take redistribution into account, the level of inequality decreases considerably, with the share going to the richest 10% dropping from 40% of primary income to a little under 30% of disposable income. Even after this adjustment, however, there remains a substantial rise in inequality over the course of the last thirty years. In the mid-

---

[1] Thomas Piketty and Emmanuel Saez, "Income Inequality in the United States, 1913–1998," *Quarterly Journal of Economics* 118, no. 1 (2003): 1–39.

Figure 2. Share of top 10% in total market income: United States, 1910–2010.

seventies, the after-tax share of the top 10% was only 23%. The American system of redistribution is only moderately cushioning the rise in primary income inequality.

The rise in primary inequality is just as conspicuous if we focus on individual wage income alone. Between the mid-1970s and the mid-1980s, the United States saw a drop in low-end wages relative to the median wage, and this trend sparked a strong debate about rising inequality. A partial remission then occurred, followed by relatively strong stability. At the same time, however, high-end wages have rocketed upward relative to the median wage. Before 1980, the top 10% were paid on average 80% more than the median wage. By 1995, this number had risen to 125%. This gap increased even more if one looks only at the highest percentiles.

The rise in inequality has led to striking disparities in the distribution of the gains from growth. U.S. Congressional

Budget Office numbers show that between 1979 and 2007—the year before the crisis—average household income (before taxes and after being adjusted for inflation) rose 150% in total. But total growth was only 37% for the poorest quintile, while it exceeded 250% for the richest 10% of the population A very large proportion of the total gains in purchasing power therefore went to the richest families. More specifically, the top 10% captured almost half of all the gains from growth over a period of thirty years and, even among this group, the top percentiles received the lion's share.

Do we see the same phenomenon taking place in other countries? The fact is, a large majority of high-income OECD countries have experienced rising income inequality over the last two decades. The Gini coefficient of disposable income per adult equivalent has risen by at least 2 percentage points in more than three-quarters of OECD countries over the last twenty years. It has even risen over 4 percentage points in a dozen or so countries. These countries include the United States, of course, but also the United Kingdom, Germany, the Netherlands, Italy, and even—and this is perhaps the most surprising given their reputation for egalitarianism—Scandinavian countries (see figure 3). It is also worth stressing that, in most of these countries, the recent economic crisis does not seem to have reversed this trend toward increasing inequality.

These variations in inequality levels might be thought to reflect changes in systems of redistribution more than changes in the distribution of primary income. However, the long-run evolution of the top income shares in market income in most high-income OECD countries is very similar to the U-shaped curve observed for the United States, although in general with some delay in the last as-

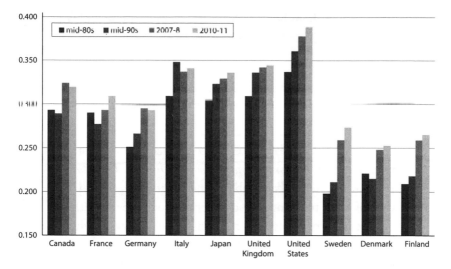

Figure 3. The increase in inequality in selected OECD countries.
Note: **Gini** coefficient of disposable income per adult equivalent, 1985–2010.

cending part.[2] On the other hand, wage inequality increased too. A recent OECD report stated that wage inequality (which is generally measured only for full-time jobs) has risen significantly in the majority of OECD countries, and "inequality has generally risen because rich households have done particularly well in comparison with middle-class families and those at the bottom of the income distribution."[3] Similarly, a study by the International Labor Organization found that two-thirds of OECD countries experienced a rise in wage inequality between 1985 and 2005, half of them because high wages pulled out even further ahead of the rest of the distribu-

[2] See the World Top Income database at http://topincomes.parisschool ofeconomics.eu/#Database.
[3] OECD, *Growing Unequal, Income Distribution and Poverty in OECD Countries* (Paris: OECD, 2008), p. 5.

tion, half of them because both the high and low ends of the distribution pulled away from the median.[4]

Exceptions

Given these statistics, it is easy to understand why two recent reports issued by the OECD on income distribution were entitled *Growing Unequal* and *Divided We Stand*. However, when talking about inequality, we should be careful not to lump all developed countries together. France is an example of a high-income country in which inequality has decreased at a fairly steady rate for a long time (at least for the period for which we have comparative statistics, which starts near the end of the 1960s). Inequalities reached their lowest levels in the mid-1990s, and these levels were low relative to other developed countries. As we can see in figure 3, inequality has nonetheless increased since then, as we have observed in other developed countries, but to a much lesser extent. An examination of the trends in wage inequality from the 1970s onward in France also leads to the same conclusion. Wage inequality among full-time workers declined steadily before rising significantly at the high end of the distribution over the very last few years, although this has not had a major effect on the synthetic measurements of inequality.

How can we explain this evolution, which seems relatively specific to France? Minimum wage laws help explain why the low end of the spectrum held steady relative to median salary. In several instances, such laws effectively caused

[4] Alexandre Kolev and Catherine Saget, "Are Middle-Paid Jobs in OECD Countries Disappearing? An Overview," *International Labor Organization,* Working Paper No. 96, 2010.

remuneration for the low end of the wage pyramid to rise faster than the rest. Another explanation is the continued rise in payroll costs, which has cut net wages at the middle and the top of the distribution more than those at the bottom, which are still protected by minimum wage laws However, it remains to be seen whether preventing the gap in wage inequality from widening came at the cost of an increase in another form of inequality: unemployment.

The example of France illustrates the differences among developed countries in the evolution of inequalities. The examples of Belgium, Spain, or Italy, in which inequalities in wages and standards of living have dropped significantly since 1990, indicate that the same trends are not at work everywhere. Eastern Europe presents a different scenario. In these countries, inequality has also grown since the first half of the 1990s due to the "transition" from socialism to a market economy. In several countries, this trend later reversed itself and inequality returned to more moderate levels.

Inequality Change in Developing Countries

Inequality in standards of living also went up in a large number of developing countries between the mid-1980s and the end of the 2000s. This is especially evident in several of the countries that are on the vanguard of the global South catching up with the North. The rise in inequality in China, where the Gini coefficient for this period increased from 0.28 to 0.42, is frequently cited as one of the black marks on its record of exceptional development. There is nothing very surprising about this, given that China is also an economy in "transition," in which inequality could only go up with market reforms. What is more significant is that, unlike most of the "transition countries" in Eastern Europe, the rise in inequality in China has continued, even accelerated, over the last several years—a full thirty years after market reforms began. What's more, this rise in inequality is uniform and it is not, as is sometimes thought, limited to an asymmetry common to the development process in which large industrial centers grow quickly and the traditional rural sector experiences relative stagnation. Rather, the rise in inequality touches all economic sectors and geographic areas. Several other large emerging Asian countries have experienced a similar rise in inequality over the recent period. This is the case with India (principally in urban areas), Indonesia, and Bangladesh. On the other hand, inequality has remained relatively stable in the rest of Asia.

We can observe the same diversity in other regions of the developing world. In Africa, some of the countries that have seen the strongest and steadiest growth have experienced a widening divergence in standards of living. This is true in particular for Ghana, Kenya, Nigeria, and the Ivory Coast prior to the 2002 crisis. In other countries the distribution has remained relatively stable (Cameroon, Uganda) or even seems to have narrowed (Senegal).

In Latin America, inequality levels have followed a clear inverted U-shaped curve over the last thirty years. They rose significantly in the 1980s as the economies were experiencing a severe balance-of-payments crisis and were submitted to draconian reforms under the "structural adjustment program" imposed by the IMF and the World Bank. This was followed by a noteworthy drop throughout the 2000s. In total, inequality has not yet returned to its earlier levels in half of all Latin American countries. In others, it has dropped below its earlier levels. Brazil, in particular, underwent a historic shift at the turn of the millennium and inequality there has been retreating substantially until reaching a level not seen since the 1960s. Nonetheless, in every country in the region, inequality levels remain substantially above inequality in any other region, except perhaps Africa.

These examples illustrate that, although there seems to be a tendency toward rising inequality in a large number of the developing economies for which sufficient data are available, there is nonetheless a significant diversity of experience. This makes identifying a general trend difficult, even if this hypothesis should not be ruled out. As the example of France and several other European countries in the developed world suggests, the presence of specific policies or institutions can prevent a rise in inequality in a given country, or can, at the very least, cushion its impact. In a similar manner, structural evolutions or cyclical shocks unique to specific countries can mask the effects of the common inegalitarian factors, either permanently or temporarily.

The Capital-Labor Split

The preceding analysis focuses on the distribution of standard of living within national populations, which is basically defined by the per person income or spending of the households in which these individuals live. It turns out that these statistics are most likely biased downward, on the one hand because they often tend to miss people at the very top of the distribution—who are not sampled or decline to answer the survey—and, on the other hand as they generally under-estimate certain kinds of income, notably income from capital or property. Personal income data also omit profits that are re-invested by companies and are therefore not distributed to households even though they constitute an implicit income for shareholders in the form of "unrealized capital gains." To the extent that those with the highest incomes tend to have a large share of their income being generated from property, the two causes for a downward bias, i.e., missing capital income and missing top income people, are closely linked to each other.[5] On the other hand, the size of the bias is most likely to change over time, so that standard income distribution data may not always catch the actual changes that take place in income inequality.

Examining the share of GDP that comes from income from property or capital can give us an idea of how this statistical bias might vary over time. It can also explain variations in individual income inequality caused by the evolution of income from capital, which this in effect takes into account. We would expect that a rise in the share of capital income in GDP would be accompanied by a rise in observed inequality, but that this rise would itself be underestimated by income distribution statistics.

It turns out that the share of corporate value added accruing to income from property has risen significantly over the course of the last thirty years in most large developed countries. Taking the G7 countries as a whole, it has increased almost continually since 1970. It was 34% in 1970 and rose to 38% by 2005. A conspicuous acceleration in

---

[5] This is a problem particularly for the statistics that come from the survey data, when they are not paired or analyzed in parallel with data from tax records.

this trend began in the late 1990s, but was halted by the 2008–2009 economic crisis.[6]

It is difficult to say whether this same phenomenon can be observed in developing countries, insofar as statistics are often unavailable and also because structural changes specific to development can influence the share of factors of production in value added. Looking solely at the manufacturing sectors of the big emerging economies, we can nonetheless observe a rising trend in the share of income from capital over the last twenty years in China, South Korea, India, Mexico, Turkey, and several other developing countries. According to recent research, the trend would actually seem to be global.[7]

This rise in the capital share of GDP leads to two conclusions. First, it is consistent with a rise in individual income inequality, specifically the kind of inequality that comes from a disproportionate rise in high-end incomes, whose earners generally draw a greater share of their income from capital than does the rest of the population. Second, it is likely that the rise in inequalities in the majority of countries that we see in the standard statistical measurements would be even more pronounced if these did not

---

[d] See OECD Employment Outlook 2012, chapter 3, or "International Monetary Fund, Spillovers and Cycles in the Global Economy," *World Economic Outlook*, April 2007, Washington, DC.

[7] For China, see Chong-En Bai and Zhenjie Qian, "Factor Income Distribution: The Story behind the Statistics," *Economic Research Journal*, Beijing, 2009, n.p.; for India, Bulet Unel, "Productivity Trends in India's Manufacturing Sectors during the Last Two Decades," IMF Working Paper, WP/03/22, January 2003; and for the other countries, Ozlem Onaran, "Wage Share, Globalization and Crisis: The Case of the Manufacturing Industry in Korea, Mexico and Turkey," *International Review of Applied Economics* 23, no. 2 (2009): 113–34. For a larger number of countries, see Loukas Karabarbounis and Breit Neiman, "The Global Decline in the Labor Share," *Quarterly Journal of Economics* (2014): 61–103.

consistently under-estimate income from capital. In particular, it would be difficult to reject the hypothesis that the recent downturn in inequality observed in the data available in Latin American countries would be substantially softened if capital income was fully taken into account.

Wealth Inequality

A concept that is related but different from income inequality, and one that is implicit to the consideration of the labor-capital split of value added, has to do with wealth, which is to say, the richness of individuals or the value of their property less outstanding debts. This inequality is less regularly tracked than wage or income inequality, which have to do with flow rather than stocks.

However, we do know, and I made this argument earlier, that the concentration of wealth far exceeds that of income. In the United States, the richest 10% receive 40% of total primary household income, but possess 71% of total wealth. For the richest 1%, the numbers are 15% and 35%, respectively. The Gini coefficient, which is around 0.38 for standard of living, rises to 0.83 for wealth. The same numbers are just as striking, although at a slightly lower level, in Europe. In France, for example, the richest 10% account for 60% of total wealth, whereas they account for only 25% of total household income. Similarly, the Gini coefficient is 0.64 for wealth, while it is only slightly above or below 0.30 for income in the recent years.

The evolution of wealth inequality over the course of the past several decades varies between countries. It has risen quite significantly in the United States, where the richest 10% have seen their share increase from 64% to

71% between 1970 and 2010, a rise that is more or less equivalent to what happened with their share of income. An almost identical rise took place in the United Kingdom, but the concentration of wealth changed only slightly in other European countries, with the notable exception of Sweden.[8]

When it comes to emerging and developing economies, we have periodic estimates of wealth distribution for only some of them. The numbers that we have show very high levels of inequality, comparable to developed countries. The Gini coefficient for wealth was estimated to be 0.55 in China, 0.65 in India, and 0.78 in Brazil and Mexico in the late 1990s or early 2000s. We know a lot less about its evolution over time. At the very least, we can think that, due to intra- and intergenerational accumulation, wealth inequality will also rise in countries in which income inequality has risen significantly. Thus, a recent study found that the Gini coefficient for wealth increased by almost 10 percentage points in China between 1995 and 2002,[9] but that India's levels were quasi-stable between 1991 and 2002.[10]

---

[8] Thomas Piketty and Gabriel Zucman report a change in the top 1% share from 22% to 24% between 1970 and 2010 in France, and from 18% to 20% in Sweden ("Wealth and Inheritance in the Long Run," in Anthony B. Atkinson and François Bourguignon, *Handbook of Income Distribution*, volume 2 (Amsterdam: Elsevier, 2014), chapter 15.

[9] Since then, and quite remarkably, it would seem that wealth inequality has drastically increased, with the Gini coefficient raising from 0.55 in 2002 to 0.76 in 2010, an order of magnitude comparable to the United States. See Shi Li, "Rising Income and Wealth Inequality in China" (http://unsdsn.org/wp-content/uploads/2014/05/TG03-SI-Event-LI-Shi-income-inequality.pdf).

[10] The numbers cited in this paragraph and the one before it are taken from James B. Davies, Susanna Sandström, Anthony B. Shorrocks, and Edward N. Wolff, "The Level and Distribution of Global Household Wealth," *Economic Journal* (March 2011): 223–54; the evolution of wealth inequal-

On the other hand, over the last several decades most developed countries have experienced a remarkable evolution in the total volume of wealth in relation to national income. In his recent book, Thomas Piketty showed how the relationship between these two numbers has changed progressively from around a 3- or 4-to-1 ratio of wealth to income directly following the Second World War, to a ratio of around 6:1 today, bringing a return to levels that existed during the eighteenth and nineteenth centuries but that were interrupted by the First World War.[11] In the future, this evolution could have important consequences with respect to inequality, for wealth as for income, in accordance with the nature of the process for the intergenerational transmission of wealth and the implications of the rising capitalization of developed economies on the capital-labor split in value added. The effects of these are probably beginning to be felt in certain countries, and not only the most advanced ones.

Non-Monetary Inequalities: Inequality of Opportunities

The inequalities that I have focused on so far have been essentially monetary ones: wage, income, standard of living, wealth. But there are also non-monetary forms of inequality—some of which can be measured and some of which cannot—that are also socially and economically significant from the point of view of both social justice and the per-

---

ity in India and China prior to 2002 was estimated by Sanjay Ruparelia et al., *Growth, Reforms and Inequality: India and China Since the 1980s*, APSA 2010 Annual Meeting Paper, 2010.

[11] Piketty, *Capital in the Twenty-First Century*.

ception that the public may have of the equity of the economy. This is the case, in particular, of the inequality of opportunities.

Two individuals or two families whose economic standards of living, measured by income or consumer spending are identical, will not necessarily feel "equal" or be considered equal in the eyes of an observer. One might have to work longer than the other or endure longer commutes and less pleasant surroundings. Because of a lack of data, trying to take these differences into account is not always easy and would not necessarily modify the conclusions based on income data about the evolution of monetary inequality. For example, correcting inequality in standards of living for disparities in hours worked between households would result in lower estimates of inequality, but the variations in this inequality over time would probably be comparable to those of monetary income inequality. Moreover, adjusting for quality of life is not always justified, insofar as this quality is often the result of trade-offs that reflect individual preferences: cheaper housing farther away from work in exchange for better vacations or, alternatively, an apartment downtown and better schools in exchange for a less expensive car.

The problem becomes more worrisome when these trade-offs are imposed on individuals and are the result of inequality of *access* to certain opportunities or activities: access to employment, credit, education, housing, for example. This is inequality of "opportunity" or, as Amartya Sen calls it, "capability."[12] These inequalities can precede inequality in standard of living and are partially responsi-

[12] See, for example, Amartya Sen, *Commodities and Capabilities* (New Delhi: Oxford University Press, 1987) .

ble for determining its magnitude. We will return to this crucial distinction between inequality in income and standard of living, or "inequality in the results" of economic activity, on the one hand, and inequality of opportunities, on the other.

Inequality of opportunity is particularly difficult to measure, in part because it is a fundamentally multidimensional concept, and in part because the opportunities open to an individual are often unobservable or un-measurable. A brief examination of some of these fundamentally nonmonetary dimensions of inequality will illustrate the nature of the problem.

Unemployment is a potentially sizable source of inequality that is only incompletely represented by statistics on income inequality. In France, for example, where unemployment has for a long time been structurally higher than in most other large developed countries, the unemployment rate has fluctuated around 9% of the labor force for two decades. However, we should also take into account underemployment, which is to say, people who are working part-time but want to work more as well as discouraged individuals who have given up trying to find a job. In total, slightly more than 4 million people, or approximately 13% of the labor force, are without employment at a given point in time, and many of these end up in this situation repeatedly and sometimes permanently. Of course, as in most developed countries, the majority of these individuals receive compensation in the form of unemployment benefits, a guaranteed minimum income, or early retirement support programs. These protections do considerably cushion the impact that unemployment has on income inequality, but they do not eliminate it. Above all, income replacement cannot compensate for the feeling of being excluded from society because you cannot get a job or for the frustration of individuals who have trouble finding and keeping a job and are at risk of having their productivity and thus their employability decline because of prolonged periods of forced economic inactivity.

Measuring the additional inequality generated by unemployment per se on top of the inequality it causes through loss of income is a difficult task. There is no obvious way of measuring the feeling of social exclusion caused by unemployment. Also, given the unemployment insurance system available in many countries, unemployment may sometimes result from individual choices rather than job rationing. Yet, it is sensible to consider that unemployment-related inequality is likely to increase with the rate of unemployment in a country. From that point of view, the situation has undoubtedly worsened in France as the structural unemployment rate, which is to say the unemployment rate corrected for cyclical fluctuations in economic activity, has increased in the past decades. Such a trend is less visible in other developed countries. As suggested previously, a relative stability in the inequality of incomes may thus have been obtained through more inequality with respect to employment.

"Employment precariousness" or the lack of a "decent job" is another aspect of non-monetary inequality. Fixed-term employment contracts, temporary work or very part-time work in developed countries, and informal jobs with irregular working hours, low earnings, and uncertain futures in developing countries are the signs of such precariousness. In France, employment precariousness has increased significantly over the last twenty years, from 8% in

1990 to 12% of total employment in the 2000s. It is possible that this rise reflects the changing preferences of a percentage of the population who favor flexible or part-time jobs and, then, could not be considered as an increase in inequality. But it could also correspond to the fact that opportunities for full-time open-ended jobs have shrunk, itself the result of a certain increase in the flexibility of employment regulations. In fact, when it comes to fixed-term contracts, employment regulations have been loosened in a large number of the OECD countries that were initially the most restrictive. Yet, if this has increased precariousness, it also may have increased employment opportunities. The overall balance for non-monetary inequality is therefore ambiguous.

Discrimination, specifically in the labor market, is another kind of inequality that is not necessarily taken into account in standard income inequality measurement. Even with identical training and professional experience, it can be more difficult for members of certain ethnic or racial groups—first- or second-generation immigrants, for example—to obtain the same job or salary than it is for "natives" or even other immigrants whose physical appearance and cultural practices are less distinctive. Women also face discrimination in the labor market. There is abundant proof of the existence of these forms of discrimination in virtually all countries, developed and developing alike. Such inequality is not necessarily reflected in the distribution of individual earnings as generally recorded, that is, without specifying who earns what. Two countries may thus have the same distribution of earnings, with the same distribution for men and women in one country and women earning systematically less than men in the other. The discrimination may also be on jobs rather than wages.

The interesting question is whether these forms of discrimination have increased in recent decades.

In most countries in the developed world, the gap between the wages of men and women has shrunk substantially since the 1970s. But, starting in the early 1990s, this convergence appears to have stabilized or at the very the least continued at a slower pace. In most countries, education differentials between men and women have virtually disappeared and, with a higher participation of women in the labor force, job experience has also equalized. The remaining wage differences across genders are thus a result of either discrimination, in a strict sense, women being paid less for strictly the same work, or remaining differences in non-observed characteristics of salaried employees.[13] In fact, some of these characteristics may also reflect individual preferences—for instance a different trade-off between family and career—on top of employers' recruitment behavior. When it comes to racial discrimination, we can see a similar development taking place in the United States, a country where this source of inequality is particularly conspicuous and where it is tracked statistically with greater precision than elsewhere. As with the gap between men and women, the rate of the reduction of racial inequality in wages has slowed since the mid-1980s, as differences in educational levels between blacks and whites have progressively declined.

---

[13] More generally, see the survey by Dominique Meurs and Sophie Ponthieux, "Gender Inequality" in Atkinson and Bourguignon (eds.), *Handbook of Income Distribution*, vol. 2, chapter 12. For the United States, see Francine Blau and Lawrence Kahn, "The U.S. Gender Pay Gap in the 1990s: Slowing Convergence," *Industrial & Labor Relations Review* 60, no. 1 (2006): 45–66.

Discrimination against migrants can be observed in most countries, even after controlling for differences in age, education, and occupation with respect to the native population or the dominant race or ethnicity. However, it is difficult to track discrimination against migrants over the long term. In fact, differences in wages have a tendency to shrink the longer migrants live in the host country and the composition of the migrant population changes with successive waves of migrants. What's more, it is often difficult to distinguish statistically between second-generation immigrants, which is to say, children of immigrants, and the children of "natives."

Differences in environment are another dimension of inequality of opportunities. Certain peri-urban zones, true "social or ethnic ghettos," bring together in a concentrated and mutually reinforcing way: first- and second-generation immigrants, youth and adult unemployment, low-quality educational facilities, and often violence and drugs. In France, 10% of the urban population lives in zones of social exclusion that are called "sensitive urban zones" (in French, *zones urbaines sensibles* or ZUS).[14] Ethnic segregation poses the same problems of safety, employment, and education in most big cities in developed countries, whether in the United States, the UK, or the Netherlands.[15] Yet, once again, it is difficult to say whether this situation has gotten worse in recent years. In France, the population living in ZUS has fallen slightly over the last twenty years, but certain

---

[14] A less literal and more accurate translation of the acronym would be something along the lines of "at-risk urban zone."

[15] See, for example, Jurgen Friedrichs, George Galster, and Sako Musterd, eds., *Life in Poverty Neighborhoods: European and American Perspectives* (London and New York: Routledge, 2005).

differences with respect to the rest of the population have had a tendency to worsen, notably in the area of education.[16]

It is difficult to assess the extent to which geographic segregation is responsible for a type of inequality that is different or similar to inequality in standards of living. Of course, a sufficient level of income would in theory allow a family to leave urban ghettos and their negative externalities. But, at the same time, it is precisely the fact of living in these disadvantaged communities that limits the opportunities of their inhabitants, or their children, to improve their economic situation.

Observed intergenerational mobility provides an idea of the difficulties that some children face due to certain characteristics of their family background, whether it be the social or ethnic groups to which they belong, their distinctive cultural traditions, or simply their parents' income. A low level of mobility implies that various obstacles have limited the access of individuals from more disadvantaged family backgrounds to higher-paid or more socially attractive careers. Few countries have the data necessary to provide us with a precise picture of the evolution of mobility over the last few decades. Overall, the available evidence suggests little or ambiguous change over time. According to some authors, intergenerational mobility diminished significantly in the United States between 1980 and 2000, after having risen during the postwar period. Yet, others find no significant changes. The comparison of two cohorts observed at the age of thirty in 1990 and 2000, respectively, suggests that intergenerational mobility could have declined in the United Kingdom. On the

[16] Corinne Chevalier and Francois Lebeaupin, "La population des zones urbaines sensibles," *Insee Première* no. 1328, December 2010.

other hand, measured in terms of the socio-professional categories of parents and children, rather than in terms of income, mobility seems either to have improved or remained stable in the countries of continental Europe over the period 1970–1990.[17]

It continues to be difficult to study intergenerational mobility in emerging and developing countries because we lack the data necessary to compare the incomes of parents and children. Several recent studies have tried to approximate inequality of opportunity by using the share of income inequality among the employed population that can be attributed to the occupational and educational situations of parents.[18] But because studies with access to sufficient data are infrequent, it is difficult to attempt to make comparisons over time.

What, then, can we conclude about the non-monetary dimensions of inequality? Taking into account the difficulty of measuring them, and even prior to that, of observing them in a way that would allow us to compare between countries and over time, our diagnosis can only be impre-

---

[17] See Daniel Aaronson and Bhashkar Mazumder, "Intergenerational Economic Mobility in the United States, 1940 to 2000," *Journal of Human Resources* 43, no. 1 (2008): 139–72, for the United States; and Jo Blanden and Stephen Machin, "Recent Changes in Intergenerational Mobility in Britain, Report for the Sutton Trust," mimeo, Center for Economic Performances, London School of Economics, 2007, for the United Kingdom. For other countries, see Richard Breen, ed., *Social Mobility in Europe* (Oxford: Oxford University Press, 2004). See also the survey by Markus Jäntti and Stephen Jenkins, "Income Mobility," in Anthony B. Atkinson and François Bourguignon, eds., *Handbook of Income Distribution*, volume 2, chapter 10.

[18] Paolo Brunori, Francisco Ferreira, and Vito Peragine, "Inequality of Opportunity, Income Inequality and Economic Mobility: Some International Comparisons," Policy Research Working Paper No. 6304, World Bank, January 2013.

cise. Nonetheless, the brief overview provided here does not reveal any strong trends that would be simultaneously occurring across a large number of countries. As for the few trends that do seem general, such as the slowing of progress in the area of wage discrimination or the increased flexibility of the labor market, interpreting these trends is still a complex task. The fact that race and gender wage gaps have stopped shrinking could be explained by a slowed convergence in non-observed factors that determine individual wages. The fact that the labor market is becoming more flexible may have increased precariousness in some jobs but also new employment opportunities, with the end result of lower unemployment.

Contrary to what we observed with income or standard of living inequality, the last two decades do not seem to have witnessed a substantial structural rise in inequality of chances or opportunities that would be general across a large number of countries. But, once again, I should emphasize that such trends would be difficult to identify, given the lack of data and the imprecision of the data that we do have.

Perceptions of Inequality

In a survey carried out in 2010 across a dozen developed and emerging countries, respondents were asked what they thought about the evolution of inequality in their own countries over the last ten years.[19] Less that 50% of Americans thought that it had increased, despite the fact that, as

[19] IFOP, "La perception des inégalités: regards croisés sur 12 pays," survey conducted for the Fondation Jean Jaurès and the Brookings Institution, http://www.ifop.com/?id=1191&option=com_publication&type=poll.

we have seen, inequality skyrocketed in the United States over that period. On the other hand, 80% of French and Dutch respondents believed that inequality had gone up in their respective countries. While this is true, inequality in those countries increased only quite slightly, and they experienced nothing like what happened in the United States. In addition, 50% of Brazilians thought that their country was becoming more unequal, despite the fact that inequality in that country, historically very high, had recently begun to experience a historic shift downward.

Such opinions should be compared alongside the conceptions these societies have about their own levels of social justice. In the same survey, a majority of Americans and Dutch reported that their societies were "just" or "fair," even though income inequality is much higher in the United States than in the Netherlands. In France, on the other hand, three-quarters of respondents said that their society was deeply unjust, despite the fact that their countries' level of inequality is similar to that in the Netherlands. When it came to this question, only Brazilians had an accurate impression of reality when they rated their society, which is objectively very unequal, as especially unjust.

There are several explanations for this divergence between subjective perceptions and objective measurements of inequalities. The first is that the conception of inequality underlying public opinion is not that of statisticians and economists; specifically, it often involves non-monetary dimensions of inequality such as those I have just discussed. For instance, it has also long been thought that American society prioritized equality of opportunity over equality of results. In other words, income inequality was considered tolerable so long as each person starts with the same chance of reaching the top of the ladder. While Bill Gates, Michael

Dell, or Madonna might contribute heavily to income inequality, in the eyes of American public opinion, they also prove that anyone can make it. The results of the 2010 survey seem to confirm that such an attitude exists. On the other hand, a recent and more detailed analysis that examined stories in the weekly news since 1980 in order to track the evolution of American public opinion on inequality suggests a much more nuanced vision, one that focuses on inequality of results as well as of opportunity, especially when these results are considered to be "undeserved."[20]

A second reason for this divergence between perception and statistical reality could be the manner in which inequality is assessed. When comparing two distributions of income or wages, one can focus either on the extremes alone or on wider groups of individuals. In other words, one could be more sensitive to the income levels of the "very rich" or the "super rich" relative to the median wage or income than one is to the proportion of total income that goes to the middle class and the poorest. And it is quite conceivable that these two perspectives might lead to contradictory conclusions. This would be the case if, for example, the share that went to the "rich" shrank in favor of both the "super rich" and the low end of the income distribution.

Looking at it from this point of view, the rise in inequality in Western societies in recent years has had a lot to do with a substantial rise in the incomes of the "super rich," even though they represent only a tiny fraction of the total population, as well as a small percentage of total income. In France, for example, if we measure inequality as the ratio

[20] Leslie McCall, *The Undeserving Rich* (Cambridge: Cambridge University Press, 2013).

between the average income of the wealthiest 10% and that of the poorest 50%, we'd find that this ratio rose from 3.7 to 3.9 between 1998 and 2007, which is an increase, of course, but a rather "moderate" one. However, if we use the richest 0.1% (one one-thousandth of the population) instead of the richest 10%, over the same time period, the ratio rises from 19 to 27, a major increase! And if we take only the richest 0.01%, inequality skyrockets, from 61 to 102. But this would only encompass approximately 3,000 households, whose share of total income is only 0.6%. Therefore, depending on whether one looks at the highest end of the distribution or a larger segment of the population, one will see either an explosive rise or a moderate increase in inequality.

It is not unlikely, given the strong influence of the media, who tend to focus on the extremes at either end of the spectrum, that public opinion can sometimes tend to exaggerate the rise in income inequality. However, even if they are sometimes incorrect or purely intuitive, perceptions of inequality and changes in these perceptions over time are important. This is partly because they reveal the limits of a purely statistical approach to inequality while suggesting implicit recognition of dimensions of economic inequality that are not sufficiently represented by measurements of a primarily monetary nature. In addition, they are important because they shape the political economy of economic reforms, starting with those that concern distribution and redistribution, but also more generally all policies that have an indirect effect on distribution. The European crisis, and the apprehensiveness certain countries in difficult situations have shown when faced with reforms that can no longer be avoided, are a good example of this. It will be difficult for the leaders of these countries to "sell" particularly painful adjustments to the public without openly cutting the exorbitant privileges built up by certain financial operators and corporate executives who, in the eyes of public opinion, are responsible for the crisis and its consequences.

Summing up, what conclusions can we draw from this brief overview of the observable facts when it comes to inequality? Besides, of course, noting the obvious rise in disparities of standards of living and salary in a large number of countries, especially developed ones, with the United States leading the pack. First of all, there are common trends in other dimensions of inequality. This is the case, for example, with the decline of the share of labor in national income or the increased precariousness of employment. Other dimensions of inequality, which are more difficult to measure, seem to have shown a greater variation in their trajectories. It is nonetheless likely that the perception of these trends in public opinion has been especially influenced by rising income inequality, in particular by the gains made by the "super-rich."

To the extent that this rise is to a certain degree uniform across countries, it seems reasonable to attribute it to common phenomena specific to recent decades. From this point of view, globalization seems the most likely candidate. It does indeed seem as if the growing openness of national economies to trade in goods and services, the movement of capital and technical know-how, and the emergence of new actors in this trade, have dramatically transformed national economies across the globe. These changes then would seem to have played a primary role in bringing about rising inequality in national economies. But, as we shall see, this rise was often the result of other factors whose connection to globalization is more indirect.

CHAPTER 3

Globalization and the Forces behind the Rise in Inequality

There are a number of forces and mechanisms that affect the distribution of income within a country. The distribution of the factors of production like human capital or wealth may change due to different accumulation behavior among people or by the public sector. The value of these factors may be modified because of changes in the relative demand for and supply of them, but also because of changes in the external economic environment of the country, in technological conditions, or in the way markets function or are regulated. Finally, changes in redistribution policy as a result of reforms in the tax and benefit system affect the distribution of disposable incomes, and, indirectly through their effect on factor prices, that of market incomes.

In trying to understand what has caused this simultaneous growth in economic inequality in a large number of countries, one might focus on exogenous changes in the environment common to all of these countries, in which case globalization and technical change are the most obvious candidates and will be examined first. But, it is also important to take into account various types of policy reforms which were undertaken simultaneously in various subsets of the countries we are considering over the last few decades, possibly in response to new common external constraints or simply through contagion. They will be analyzed in the second part of this chapter.

To the extent that globalization enables better integration primarily of the developing world into the global economy, one might expect that its potential distributive effects have been different in developed and developing economies. As this also applies to the nature of policy reforms and the circumstances in which they have been undertaken, care will be taken throughout the chapter to distinguish the two sets of countries.

The Effects of Globalization and Deindustrialization on Developed Countries

The 1980s and early 1990s witnessed a radical change in the world economy. Whole swaths of the world were opened up to international trade, most importantly China in the 1980s and the Soviet bloc and India at the turn of the 1990s. Simple economic reasoning suggests that the opening up of these giants to international trade was equivalent to the entrance of around a billion workers, for the most part unskilled, into international competition, with the simultaneous effect of creating a relative scarcity of other factors of production, particularly capital, skilled labor, and raw materials. The relative remuneration for these factors and the share they represented in national incomes rose throughout the world, while the share and relative remuneration of unskilled labor diminished.

The global competition created by the entrance of these new players into world markets was not only facilitated by direct investment from the developed economies, but also was reinforced by increased competition within developed economies as a result of deregulation, the liberalization of trade and, in Europe, the introduction of the "single market." By drastically reducing the relative cost of transportation, technological progress also made the growing fragmentation of international value chains possible, which lowered production costs via subcontracting, thus reinforcing the process of geographical reallocation of global production activities.

This simple view of the effect of the entrance of these new players in global trade fits the simplest form of the economic theory of international trade, often referred to as the Heckscher-Ohlin model. The opening up of countries with such abundant unskilled labor forces inevitably led to the expansion of global trade, with these countries exporting unskilled labor-intensive goods and countries that are relatively abundant in capital, that is, developed countries or the so-called North, specializing in capital- and technology-intensive goods. In other words, the geographical allocation of production had to evolve with labor-intensive sectors moving toward developing countries and developed countries specializing more in goods and services that are intensive in capital, skilled labor, and technology. Assuming that factor markets are reasonably competitive, the distribution of income would thus move away from unskilled labor in favor of the other factors of production in the North, with the opposite occurring in the South.

At first sight, rough evidence seems in agreement with this simple model. Indeed, it is clear today that the volume of global trade has surged and that globalization has resulted in a large share of the production of exchangeable (or "tradable") goods that require intensive use of unskilled labor being relocated in emerging economies. In developed countries, this labor is now concentrated around services that are protected from international competition, such as construction, personal service, and hospitality in hotels or restaurants. On the distributive side, it seemed for a while as if the globalization of exchange would mostly impact the wages of the least skilled workers, who would be exposed to competition from cheap labor. This is exactly how some people interpreted the drop in real wages of unskilled labor in the United States in the 1980s and the persistence of high levels of unemployment in Europe. An American economist at the time even asked if the wages for this type of labor were not "being set in Beijing."[1] Another distributive change in agreement with this simple theory is the observeable increase in the share of capital in the total income of advanced countries, as discussed in the preceding chapter.

Other changes, however, have taken place in the global economy over recent decades that go somewhat beyond

---

[1] Richard Freeman, "Are Your Wages Set in Beijing?", *Journal of Economic Perspectives* 9, no. 3 (1995): 15–32.

the simple economic model of trade and globalization. Take for example the relative loss of real earnings at the middle of the skill ladder that is being observed in several countries. Indeed, as was mentioned in the previous chapter, in both the United States and the UK it is not only the bottom of the earning distribution but also its middle part, around the median, that has lost in comparison with the mean in the recent decades, despite the fact that workers in that part of the distribution are already skilled—almost 50% of the employed labor force in the United States has the equivalent of a bachelor's degree or more. A possible explanation of such a change lies in advances in information and communication technology that led to a growing number of back office tasks—which require a certain level of skill—being outsourced to emerging economies through increasingly efficient data transfer technology (e.g., accounting, statistical monitoring, software development). This evolution may have led to a reduction in demand, and therefore in the relative remuneration of these workers in developed countries. Since the demand for higher skilled workers remains strong, the result is that the wage distribution became more skewed, to the detriment of low and medium skills and to the benefit of higher skills and presumably capital.[2]

In short, the opening up of large countries with sizable unskilled or moderately skilled labor forces to international trade has resulted in a reallocation of productive activity in the world which has, in turn, led to a two-stage evolution of the wage ladder in developed countries. First, wages at

[2] Maarten Goos, Alan Manning, and Anna Salomons, "Explaining Job Polarization in Europe: The Roles of Technology, Globalization and Institutions," Centre for Economic Performance, LSE, CEP Discussion Papers, no. 1026, 2010.

the low end of the scale lost out relative to the rest, because they faced competition from the massive increase in the amount of unskilled labor available in developing countries. In the second stage, it was those in the middle who were especially affected by increased competition in intermediary service activities. The low end of the distribution therefore gained relative to the middle, while the middle and bottom both lost ground relative to the top. In addition to this phenomenon, the relative rise in remuneration for factors of production other than labor, the result of the expansion of international trade and the restructuring of production in developed economies, has tended to favor the owners of these factors, who are generally located at the high end of the ladder, often at the very top.

This rather simple picture of the effects of international competition on wage distribution fits pretty well with what we've been able to observe in countries such as the United States and the UK since the early 1980s. In other developed countries, however, the first phase was cushioned by a greater rigidity of low-end wages given the functioning of the labor market. And yet, as we will see later on, it would be a gross oversimplification to attribute the observed evolution of wage inequality solely to the geographic restructuring of global production.

We must also reject the commonly held view that the current phase of accelerated globalization has generally impoverished developed economies to the benefit of emerging economies. In general, both groups won in the expansion of trade. For the emerging economies, there is little doubt that the opening up of markets contributed to rapid growth given that it opened enormous outlets for their production and accelerated gains in productivity, partly in connection with foreign direct investment. In developed countries, while certain sectors of the economy have suffered in the face of new competition, some others, notably goods and services that are capital-, skill-, or technology-intensive, have benefited; others still have been sheltered from new foreign competition, principally some service sectors. In addition, prices for a large number of goods, which are now imported, have gone down, contributing to a noticeable rise in purchasing power. Of course, these gains were unequally distributed within national economies, and certain social groups have profited more than others—some have even been harmed—but taken as a whole, the net economic effect looks positive.

Beyond its effect on wages, another source of inequality that is linked to the globalization of trade has been the increased precariousness of employment resulting from such large-scale economic readjustment. Partly due to the influence of new competition from emerging economies, since 1980 the share of manufacturing in total jobs has been halved in the United States, more than halved in the UK, and slightly less in France. It has even fallen by about a third in Germany, the bastion of European manufacturing. In some countries, which in the past we would have called "industrialized," this sector now represents little more than 10% of total labor, sometimes even less; thirty years ago it would have employed 20–30%. Of course, there are other reasons that explain this decline, such as technological progress, which has been faster in manufacturing than elsewhere, as well as changes in the structure of consumption in favor of services. Nonetheless, there are two crucial points I would like to emphasize. First, a retreat of this size would not have been possible without the expansion of trade with less industrialized economies, particularly with the emerging countries in Asia. Second, such changes could only have had a negative impact on job stability, first in manufacturing itself, but also in the service sector to which excess labor will turn for employment.

Thus, the problem is less "offshoring" than the closing of units or lines of production that had become uncompetitive and the creation of new economic activities in countries with low labor costs. Of the 70,000 jobs lost on average every year by the French manufacturing sector between 1980 and 2007, less than 10% are attributable to direct offshoring to emerging countries, while more than 30% can be attributed to international competition in general (for instance the closure of production lines rather than relocating them, and the creation of new activities overseas rather than on national territory), 30% to gains in productivity and a decline in domestic demand, and 30% to the subcontracting of certain jobs to the service sector, including temporary contract work.[3] It is important to point out, however, that these various factors are not independent of one another. Specifically, gains in productivity are in part an indirect effect of globalization, as they are a way of confronting competition in whatever form it might take by reducing the amount of labor necessary for a given amount of productive output. In France, the number of jobs per constant euro of industrial production today is one-sixth of what it was twenty-five years ago.

In conclusion, even if, strictly speaking, the phenomenon of offshoring has had only a limited effect on industrial employment, there is no doubt that globalization accelerated the deindustrialization of developed countries and led to the increased precariousness of employment in

[3] See Lilas Demmou, "La désindustrialisation en France" (document de travail de la DG Trésor, 2010/01, Paris, 2010).

the regions on which it has had the greatest impact. It is also undoubtedly the case that, at present, competition from low-wage countries in some services employing medium-skilled labor is increasing, a process that is being reinforced by technological advances.

Globalization from a
Southern Perspective

The impact globalization has had on emerging economies is radically different from what has been observed in developed countries. While the growth of exports made possible by the expansion of trade, often with the support of foreign investment from rich countries, has been a major factor in development, the link between the opening up of these economies and the evolution of inequality is far less clear.

In these countries, the process of development itself as much as the globalization of trade has led to the restructuring and modernization of their economies. That said, there is no doubt that the export of manufactured goods to rich countries has been a powerful force for development in China and other Asian countries, as was the case in the 1960s and 1970s for the Asian "dragons" (South Korea, Hong Kong, Singapore, and Taiwan).

From a distributive point of view, the economic restructuring caused by the globalization of trade in developing countries has taken place in a much more favorable direction than it has in developed ones. First of all, it has led to a transfer of jobs from low-productivity agricultural or artisanal sectors to a better paid industrial sector, situated toward the higher end of the distribution, though not at the very top. In the "dragons," this process took place without having a major impact on income distribution. Over the last decades, however, inequality has risen in China and India while these countries have continued to develop at a fast pace, although it is important to note that other forces were also at work here. In China, the transition from a socialist economy to a market economy could only increase inequality. Over the more recent period, the rapid accumulation of fortunes by a nascent entrepreneurial class, as well as the increased demand for skilled labor, have contributed to a greater concentration of income. To this we can add geographical disequilibria, which are more or less inherent to the process of economic development, that tend to favor certain regions and cities over others. There is evidence that interregional income inequality has substantially increased in China since the beginning of the reforms in 1980.[4] The same phenomena are also present in India. The deregulation of what was essentially a planned economy, the opening up to trade and foreign investment and the development gap between urban and rural areas, have contributed to a sizable increase in income inequality.

This rise in inequality in countries that have begun exporting goods that require intensive unskilled labor seems to contradict standard international trade theory. As seen earlier, the basic model holds that, because the demand for their labor will increase, the unskilled labor force should be the prime beneficiary of this change.[5] But in developing countries with a substantial labor surplus, wages in indus

---

[4] A detailed decomposition may be found in Tun Lin, Juzhong Zhuang, Damaris Yarcia, and Feng Lin, "Income Inequality in the People's Republic of China and Its Decomposition: 1990–2004," *Asian Development Review* 25 (2008): 119–36.

[5] This is the so-called Stolper-Samuelson theorem of the neoclassical theory of international trade.

trial export sectors are largely set exogenously at higher levels than the competitive level, that is to say, the remuneration in the agriculture or artisanal sectors, which therefore serve as a limitless pool (a "reserve army") of labor. The expansion of the export sector can therefore take place without any direct impact on industrial wages, primarily benefiting on the one hand the workers newly engaged in manufacturing and, on the other hand, capital-owners. Such a scenario, which is compatible with a rise, rather than a drop, in inequality, provides a relatively accurate description of what has happened in the Chinese economy over the last several decades.

All in all it may therefore be that capital has been the main beneficiary of the globalization of trade and the resulting acceleration in economic growth that has taken place over the last two decades. In developed countries, this evolution has contributed to a greater specialization in goods whose production requires more capital, increasing both its relative scarcity and its remuneration.[6] The preceding argument suggests that capital may have also been the main beneficiary in emerging countries that are exporting labor-intensive manufactured products. As for the majority of developing economies that, despite the globalization process, keep exporting mostly raw materials, whether agricultural or mineral, it is again capital- and large property-owners (sometimes the state) who profited from rising demand and prices for these basic commodities. Last, at the

---

[6] For a measurement of the role globalization has played in the rise of capital's share in national income, see Florence Jaumotte and Irina Tytell, "How Has the Globalization of Labor Affected the Labor Income Share in Advanced Countries?" IMF Working Paper, WP/07/298, Washington, DC, 2007.

global level, the investments multinationals have made in emerging countries where labor is cheap and in the extraction sectors of natural resource–rich countries have also contributed to a rise in their profit margins.

There is nothing really surprising about this generalized relative increase in capital income. Raising profits is obviously the essential motor of globalization itself, whether in developed countries, in developing countries, or at the global level. In any event, this has probably been a major factor in explaining the rise observed in a large number of countries in the share of income that goes to capital and the richest section of the population, as discussed in the preceding chapter.

Overall, globalization has thus most likely played a role in increasing inequality in most countries over the recent decades, although its impact will have varied depending on the country considered and each one's specific context or policies. Yet, there are still other forces that have played a part in modifying the distribution of income, which we turn to now.

Technological Progress, Superstars, Bosses, and Very High Incomes

The vertiginous development of communication and information science and technology has profoundly transformed the modes of production of goods and services, while creating an increased demand for workers who know how to use these new technologies. As with the increased specialization in capital- and skill-intensive goods brought about by globalization, this transformation has contributed to a rise in the relative remuneration of skilled labor in developed countries.[7] But the very facts of globalization and of the spontaneous international spread of innovations have meant that this same phenomenon has been at work in developing economies too and represents another possible explanation for rising inequalities in these countries.

We often treat technological progress as if it were a completely exogenous force that transformed production techniques and therefore altered the demand for their factors and the remuneration of these factors. But it can also be seen, at least partly, as a product of globalization itself. To the extent that competition is a major engine of innovation, we cannot fail to recognize that by intensifying competition between companies that operate in global markets, the expansion of world trade has accelerated the pace of technological innovation and its effects on remuneration scales.

There are also reasons to think that technological innovation per se, rather than the additional income or profit it generates, is to a certain extent responsible for the explosion of very high incomes in many countries. Let us take a look at a few examples of this.

The development of communications technology has greatly multiplied the possible audience size for artists, writers and athletes. Enrico Caruso, who was, thanks to the invention of the record, the first opera singer to become an international star, sold around a million records. About a century later, Luciano Pavarotti sold more than a hundred

---

[7] In fact, economists have spent a great deal of time studying the question of whether the rise in inequalities observed in the 1980s was primarily attributable to the expansion of trade or technological progress. See, for example, the revisiting of this debate by Paul Krugman, "Trade and Wages Reconsidered," *Brookings Papers on Economic Activity* (2008): 103–54.

million. In the past, singers could perform only before limited audiences in enclosed spaces if they still wanted to be
heard. On their last world tour, the rock band U2 played
more than a hundred concerts in stadiums and other public spaces, with an average audience size of 40,000! It's not
difficult to see how the income of these artists has risen
relative to the income of less talented artists, who are often
happy if they make a basic living from their art.

We can observe the same phenomenon with regard to
movies, television, publishing, and sports. J. K. Rowling,
the author of the Harry Potter books, receives an annual
income of some $300 million, while 90% of English-
language authors earn less than $80,000 annually. The
Swedish soccer player Zlata Ibrahimovich earns more than
15 million euros per year in the Paris Saint-Germain soccer
team, thirty times more than the average player in the
French Ligue 1. The number of people willing to pay any
sum in order to catch a glimpse of these stars, and the vast
amounts of money that companies will offer them to ad-
vertise their goods and thus reach out to their huge fan
bases, are also significant sources of income. These superstars represent a significant segment of the very high income bracket. They have technological advances to thank
for their superstar status, as these have allowed them to
reach a truly global audience. Technical progress and globalization also explain the development of "winner-take-
all" dynamics.[8]

The same phenomena of scale explain the recent emergence of other "very high incomes." In the financial sector,
skilled financial operators are awarded bonuses at the end

[8] Robert H. Frank, *The Winner-Take-All Society: Why the Few at the
Top Get So Much More Than the Rest of Us* (New York: Penguin Books,
1995).

of the year that are more or less proportional to the profits they generated for their company. Advances in communication and information technology have increased the volume of financial operations and made it possible for a single person to manage a huge portfolio, often worth a few billion dollars, and to generate larger profits. This has catapulted a relatively large percentage of traders into the very high income bracket.

This also explains the enormous rise in the remuneration of the heads of large companies, which is so often in the news. It is striking that the remuneration of executives correlates so closely with the size of the companies that they run. So the heads of the ten largest American companies are compensated around four times as much as the heads of companies that were close to the 100th place in terms of size. In France, this ratio is around 3, slightly below Germany. It is just as remarkable that the increase in the size of big companies (or "multinationals") over the last two or three decades has been accompanied by a parallel rise in the relative remuneration of their directors in comparison to smaller companies.[9]

If the growing size of big companies partly explains the surge in executive remuneration, the question of whether these salaries reflect real talent is open to debate. The argument that enormous salaries of several million euros or dollars are necessary incentives for CEOs to perform at a higher level seems rather specious. There is certainly a grain of truth to this argument, but it is hard not to think that

[9] See Xavier Gabaix and Augustin Landier, "Why Has CEO Pay Increased So Much?" *Quarterly Journal of Economics* 123, no. 1 (2008): 49–100; for a more general approach, see Frédéric Palomino, *Comment faut-il payer les patrons?* Paris, "Collection du Cepremap," Éditions rue d'Ulm, 2011.

these salaries also reflect the acquisition of informational rents by senior management, as well as effects of contagion or imitation among firms. It is also possible that, over time, these practices have become established as new social norms, weakening the link between remuneration and true executive productivity. Moreover, this rise in executive remuneration is a relatively recent phenomenon. Remuneration of U.S. executives was remarkably stable and relatively low in the postwar period up until the 1970s. In comparison with the average earnings in their company, CEOs' compensations were forty times higher. In 2005, this ratio was above 100. Yet several of the biggest U.S. companies expanded internationally at a very fast rate in the 1960s and 1970s.[10]

Within these large companies, the rise in executive remuneration has also spread to include other high-level corporate officers as well as CEOs, and this is also true of other sectors. In the financial sector, it would be difficult for the trading floor manager to make less money than one of his traders, and, of course, the remuneration for an executive officer cannot very well be lower than that of a trading floor manager. Another way in which these very high salaries spread comes from the provision of specialized services to superstars or multinational corporations. For example, lawyers who take part in litigation involving large sums of money will often be compensated directly in proportion to

[10] Carola Frydman and Raven Saks, "Executive Compensation: A New View from a Long-Term Perspective, 1936–2005," *Review of Financial Studies* 23, no. 5 (2010): 2099–2138. In *Capital in the Twenty-First Century*, Thomas Piketty relates the explosion in top executives' pay to the drop in top marginal income tax rates in the 1980s, the argument being that it was not worth negotiating a high level of compensation when 70% would go to the state. I'll return to the tax issue later.

the sums in question. Certain law firms have therefore seen their fees skyrocket just like those of the superstars they work for, and the net effect of this process of contagion has made a significant impact on income distribution.

The explosion of very high incomes has not been restricted to developed economies alone. Technological advances and the expanding size of markets have also led to an amazing rise in the salaries of Bollywood celebrities and cricket stars relative to their fellow Indian citizens, as well as an increase in the number of Chinese billionaires.

Another phenomenon that also stems from globalization and is linked to the emergence of the super rich is taking place in developing countries as well as developed ones: the increased international mobility of the highest skilled workers and a resulting homogenization of international standards of remuneration. Take the example of an African president looking for a finance minister. Where better to look for the most qualified candidate than among fellow nationals employed by the IMF, the World Bank, or Wall Street? Of course, recruiting someone like that will require a salary that is more or less equivalent to what that person could make abroad. What's more, once the minister accepts the position, the question arises of the remuneration of his chief of staff and assistants, given that their pay cannot be all that much lower, which means that it will be significantly higher than what their similarly qualified fellow countrymen would earn. This is how the fluidity of the global high-skilled labor market has led to a certain kind of contagion between countries at the high end of the income ladder. French traders can raise the possibility of moving to London in order to receive remuneration similar to London traders' salaries, and German or Swedish CEOs can threaten their shareholders that they will move to a partner company in the United States. Yet, it is worth noting that big differences still do exist between countries. The best paid CEOs in the United States still earn around four times what the best paid German CEOs earn in companies of comparable size.

Institutions versus Markets

The explanations for rising inequality that I've summarized so far are all directly tied to market mechanisms. Certain shocks—technological advances, the development of trade, the opening up of emerging markets—have hit the global economy and national economies, modifying the quantity of goods and services exchanged or produced, as well as affecting employment, prices, and wages. These mechanisms themselves operate within a given institutional environment, at both the national and international levels. But over recent decades, this environment itself has changed, leading on the one hand to changes in the disposable incomes through reforms of the tax-benefit system, and on the other hand to changes in the way markets operate and therefore in the distribution of market income.

The defining institutional change in the last quarter of the twentieth century was undoubtedly the deregulation of markets and the process of economic liberalization, launched at the end of the 1970s in the United States by the Reagan administration and in the United Kingdom by the Thatcher government. This would later spread to the rest of the world, with a significant acceleration after the fall of the Berlin Wall in 1989. These reforms sought to relax what were seen as the overly strict regulations that states had placed on markets in the aftermath of the financial crisis of the 1930s and the Second World War, and to liberate individual initiative from what were seen as stifling levels of taxation and regulation. The economic climate—national economies were adapting to a changing world economy, which had just undergone its first major postwar shock with the oil price crises of the 1970s—made the implementation of these reforms politically feasible. They then spread to the majority of the developed world and subsequently, as a result of the debt crisis of the 1980s, to a good portion of the developing world.

In the following subsections, I will summarize the major principles of these reforms in developed countries.

Taxation

From the perspective of distribution, the most important reforms were the changes in taxation, particularly the income tax cuts. The justification given for these was that the marginal tax rates on the highest incomes were practically confiscatory and were discouraging entrepreneurship and investment, while incentivizing tax evasion and "optimization." Lower tax rates were intended to restore these incentives and reduce tax evasion while maintaining tax revenue at its existing levels. The highest marginal tax rate fell from 70% to 40% in the United States during the Reagan administration. In the United Kingdom, it plummeted from 83% to 60% in the very first year of the Thatcher government while, simultaneously, the value added tax rose from 6% to 15%, all in all a deeply regressive reform. Later, several other countries would adopt similar, albeit not quite as far-reaching, measures: Germany in 1986–1990, then again in 2003; France in 1986 and 2002. A dramatic example of this was Sweden's "tax reform of the century" in

1991. In this traditionally egalitarian country with a strongly redistributive tax system, the highest marginal income tax rate dropped from 70% to 45%, while the indirect tax rate was increased to compensate for at least part of the revenue lost. As in the United Kingdom, inequality rose substantially.

Changes in the highest marginal income tax rates are only a part of the picture of the tax reforms carried out in the name of economic liberalization. An important dimension of these reforms, one that was itself tied to the growing mobility of capital in the context of globalization, was the introduction of the distinction between the taxation of income from capital and savings and the taxation of income from labor. Over time a dual system evolved in which income from savings was taxed at non-progressive flat rates which were intended to be more or less similar across countries and were in any event lower than the highest marginal tax rates on income from labor. As the share of income from capital tends to increase as income increases, average tax rates for the very high income brackets ended up actually falling. This was true in France, the United States, and the majority of developed countries.[11] In the same vein, tax rates on corporate profits were also reduced in the majority of developed economies, with the obvious result that direct taxation has become less progressive. In the United States, for example, an analysis that took into account the federal taxes on income, profits, inheritance and payroll costs showed that the effective tax rate on the richest 1% dropped by around 15 percentage points between 1970 and 2004, often dropping below that paid by the middle classes.[12]

[11] See Camille Landais, Thomas Piketty, and Emmanuel Saez, *Pour une révolution fiscale* (Paris: La République des Idées/Seuil, 2011).
[12] Thomas Piketty and Emmanuel Saez, "How Progressive Is the U.S.

At the other end of the scale, there has not been a general cutting of redistribution to the lowest-income segment of the population, although such cuts have taken place in a few countries. The welfare state in the United Kingdom faced serious cuts under the Thatcher government, and the economic crisis in Sweden in the early 1990s led the country to reform its system of social protections. In both of these cases, the reforms led to rising inequality on top of a less progressive taxation system. In other countries, social spending has rarely been reduced. On the contrary, spending has tended to increase due to factors, such as a growing aging population and worsening employment situation, which have made programs that offer support to the long-term unemployed and low-income individuals ever more necessary. In fact, the percentage of GDP going to social programs has increased in the majority of OECD countries.

Privatization and Deregulation

Outside of taxation, the deregulatory movement undertaken in the 1980s had other consequences that might account in part for rising inequality. It is difficult to summarize the total distributive effect of the wave of privatizations that swept over Europe, starting in Great Britain, and of all the policies that were intended to increase competition in the United States and Europe. Some of these policies resulted in efficiency gains that sometimes translated into better services and lower prices for everyone, and sometimes reduced monopoly rents that had benefited the

Federal Tax System? A Historical and International Perspective," *Journal of Economic Perspectives* 21, no. 1 (2007): 1–24.

wealthiest. But placing certain public companies under private control often led to a profound restructuring of their activity, the number of people they employed, and their geographic footprint, which in turn had dramatic effects on particular social groups and regions.

Two kinds of measures deserve a more in-depth analysis, given that they have had a clear and significant impact on distribution: financial deregulation and the deregulation of the labor market.

THE DEREGULATION AND GLOBALIZATION OF FINANCE

The boom in the financial sector that characterized the last two or three decades was the result of several factors. At the macroeconomic level, the disinflation that took place at the beginning of the 1980s re-energized financial markets by eliminating a major source of uncertainty about the cost of and the real return on capital. This disinflation occurred alongside the deregulation of financial market operations, based on re-establishing competition among operators of all kinds and the computerization of markets, and led to the 1986 "Big Bang" of the City in London. The success of these reforms, which could be seen in the impressive development of the City, led to them being adopted first in the United States and then in continental Europe, where they were facilitated by the growing openness of international financial markets. This change was particularly conspicuous in France, where, until the late 1980s, financial mechanisms remained constrained by very rigid regulatory systems based on a few large nationalized banks and the strict regulation of foreign exchange operations.

The development of the financial sector might have had an effect on economic inequality in several ways and in several directions, but it is not easy to judge what its total impact was, especially in the aftermath of a major crisis whose causes themselves were partly linked to this development. That said, I will nonetheless attempt to identify the channels through which the evolution of this sector influenced income distribution in developed countries over recent decades.

A rather simplistic line of argument might suggest that financial liberalization, by making the allocation of available funds more competitive between lenders and by facilitating the access of financially constrained agents to credit, both improved the efficiency of the economy as a whole and contributed to the development of sectors and businesses that were initially deprived of access to credit. This latter effect would significantly benefit the small and midsized entrepreneurs and the labor they recruit from the lower end of the income ladder. At the same time, we might think that by increasing the demand for credit, and financial capital in general, liberalization also increased its remuneration, which would naturally benefit the high end of the scale. Based on this simple theoretical interpretation, the total impact would seem to be ambiguous.[13]

But financial liberalization has had other effects that have been more clearly inegalitarian. Even if the initial aim was to encourage competition, today the financial sector as a whole is clearly oligopolistic, if only because of economies of scale in financial intermediation, which are themselves partly tied to innovations in information and communications technology. The existence of substantial rents and the nature of the financial sector's activities have made

[13] For a review of the ties between the development of finance and income distribution, see Asli Demirguc-Kunt and Robert Levine, "Finance and Inequality: Theory and Evidence," *Annual Review of Financial Economics* 1 (2009): 287–318.

possible the very high incomes of certain operators and executive officers, via the microeconomic mechanisms described earlier. And, in fact, the overrepresentation of the financial sector among very high incomes is remarkable. In the United States, 13% of very high incomes are connected to the financial sector, this number being 18% in France and the UK, even though this sector represents only 5% of total jobs.[14]

The rise in CEOs' and top executives' compensation is also linked to the development of the financial sector. The increasing "financialization" of economies has made them more sensitive to the annual performance of companies. Share price as an indicator of the value of a company plays a far more important role than it did in the past. Because of this, shareholders have tended to be willing to offer higher remuneration to executives, either directly or indirectly through stock options and other mechanisms, in an effort to obtain the best possible results. At the same time, this quest for profitability has also contributed to shortening the horizon of investors and managers, at the cost of weaker social, and probably even private, profitability over the long term.

Empirically determining the end result of these various effects is difficult, given that generally what we can observe is the direct effect of a given policy of liberalization on its direct beneficiaries over the short or medium term, rather

[14] See Mike Brewer, Luke Sibieta, and Liam Wren-Lewis, *High Income Individuals: Racing Away?* (London: Institute for Fiscal Studies, 2008) for the United Kingdom; Michel Amar, "Les très hauts salaires du secteur privé," *INSEE première* no. 1288 (April 2010) for France; and Jon Bakija, Adam Cole, and Bradley Heim, "Jobs and Income Growth of Top Earners and the Causes of Changing Income Inequality: Evidence from U.S. Tax Return Data" (mimeo, Williams College, 2012) for the United States.

than its long-term effects once they have spread to the economy as a whole. A few examples of natural experiments are interesting. Take the gradual bank deregulation in the United States that took place from the mid-1970s to 1994. It allowed banks headquartered in one state to open branches in others, increasing the degree of competitiveness in this sector. Taking advantage of the fact that this liberalization took place in stages over time, which allowed them to compare states where it had taken place with states where it had not yet been implemented, Beck, Levine, and Levkov were able to find that a statistically significant drop in income inequality followed this financial liberalization.[15]

Should we conclude from this that financial liberalization, whatever it might be, contributes to income equality? Far from it. The deregulation in question was of a very specific kind and was neither directly related to the development of new financial products nor connected with the explosion in the international mobility of capital. These probably represent the two trends that contributed to most of the rise in very high incomes that we can observe across the globe, in part by increasing the profitability of financial wealth through an outsized expansion of investment opportunities and in part by inflating the remunerations of the small number of people who were directing and managing these innovations.

And how could we forget that the second type of deregulation (new financial products and the increased fluid-

---

[15] Thorsten Beck, Robert Levine, and Alexey Levkov, "Big Bad Banks? The Winners and Losers from Bank Deregulation in the United States," *Journal of Finance* 65, no. 5 (2010): 1637–67. See also the other references to this natural experiment in Demirguc-Kunt and Levine, "Finance and Inequality."

ity of the international mobility of capital) were directly implicated in the recent financial crisis, the economic recession that followed, and the disastrous effect this has had on the incomes of a large segment of the population, not always those at the top end of the income scale?

In conclusion, we cannot ignore the fact that certain aspects of the financial liberalization initiated in the mid-1980s in developed countries influenced the equality of income distribution in a positive direction. Other aspects of this process, however, clearly were also responsible for a significant rise in very high incomes, which is the dominant feature of current trends in inequality. Ultimately, it is also possible that its effects were negative for the lower end of the distribution if we admit that poorly regulated financial liberalization was the primary cause of the current "great recession."

THE DEREGULATION OF THE LABOR MARKET

The labor market has also been a major target for deregulatory policies. The OECD has created an indicator of the strictness of employment protection policies that combines different measures of the intensity of the constraints imposed by employment legislation on several aspects of work: restrictions on and costs for dismissing individuals or groups of employees with permanent contracts, the regulation of fixed-term or temporary contract work (length, number of renewals allowed), and so forth. Of twenty OECD countries, fourteen have relaxed these regulations over the last twenty years, including many in Northern Europe. The Anglo-Saxon countries are not among the reformers, but regulation in these countries is already far less restrictive than elsewhere. France is one of the rare countries in which, according to the OECD, the employment protection laws have become stronger over this period, albeit only slightly.

There are various other ways besides these employment protection laws that the labor market is regulated, including through the role of unions and collective bargaining, social contributions, or wage deductions, and payroll charges imposed on employees and employers, unemployment compensation and, of course, minimum wage laws. It turns out that in a large number of developed countries, one or more of these methods for regulating the labor market have been significantly reformed over the last twenty or thirty years. Economists have studied these reforms closely, hoping to understand their effects and to ascertain whether these effects were what policymakers had anticipated, specifically with respect to questions of inequality and employment.

From a theoretical point of view, policies regulating the labor market will generally have an a priori ambiguous effect on employment and inequality. More often than not, the direct positive effects of deregulation are accompanied by indirect effects that can often counteract its initial aims. I will provide a few examples of these counterproductive mechanisms, and then I will examine the question of the extent to which empirical analysis can lift the ambiguity as to the direction or size of the effects of these regulatory changes.

We can see how employment protection policies can improve motivation and productivity by making employees feel that their position is less precarious, which benefits employers as well. Beyond a certain point, however, these regulations increase the net cost of labor by restricting employers' room to maneuver. These excessive costs have repercussions on the total volume of employment and can potentially result in an unequal dual labor market. In such a scenario, there is a protected sector that is difficult for outsiders to access due to low job turnover, and there is an unprotected sector where employers attempt to use all of the tools allowed by the law to circumvent employment regulations, such as resorting to temporary contracts, for example. This dualism in terms of employment is reflected by a dualism in wages. The protected sector is generally more productive, so, in part because of these protections, its employees are better remunerated. It is therefore necessary to balance the inequality produced by lack of protection and the resulting insecurity of employement, whose effects can potentially be limited by effective unemployment insurance (as with the Danish "flexicurity" system), against the wage inequality produced by a dual labor market. It is not clear that the countries that went in the direction of the first option by deregulating their labor markets necessarily ended up with increased inequality as a result.

Other labor market institutions have a more direct impact on inequality. The first of these I will examine will be collective bargaining for wages and the role of unions. Nearly all developed economies, with the exception of those in Belgium and some Scandinavian countries, have seen a conspicuous drop in the power of unions and a commensurate decrease in the role of collective bargaining. There are several explanations for this evolution. There was, of course, the fact that certain governments, like those of Reagan and Thatcher, were hostile to union activity—which, as we remember, was played out rather spectacularly with regard to air traffic controllers in one case and miners in the other. But this explanation is not sufficient; the causes behind the decline of unions are deeper. From an economic perspective, there are three main causes: increased competition in markets for goods and services, economic restructuring, and disinflation. The competition created by globalization and the deregulation of national economies gradually rendered obsolete the model of unions negotiating head to head with employers. Over time, competition eroded existing rents and therefore management's room to maneuver and the negotiating power of unions. At the same time, deindustrialization was shrinking the most traditional sphere of labor union activity, pushing unions into making major structural changes. And, finally, disinflation radically reduced the utility of collective bargaining in determining salary levels. In a high-inflation world, workers and employers find it difficult to negotiate on an individual basis, without explicit reference to the way other workers' salaries are adjusted for inflation, which creates a clear opportunity for the unions to coordinate wage negotiations. In a low-inflation world, on the contrary, personal characteristics and performances are easier to take into account in individual wage negotiations.

Government-mandated minimum wage laws are another tool for counteracting labor market forces and limiting income inequality, or at the very least wage inequality. Most developed countries have such laws, even if some of them allow collective bargaining to determine the minimum wage for specific sectors of the economy. The impact of a legal minimum on wage inequality nonetheless depends on whether it follows or precedes productivity gains in the economy. In this respect, we can observe a certain degree of variation within OECD countries. Since 1980, in countries like the United States, Belgium, Spain, or the Netherlands, the minimum wage has declined relative to the average or the median wage. On the other hand, it has increased in France, Japan, and the UK (where it was only introduced in 1999).[16]

As with employment protection laws, the effects of unionization and minimum wage laws on income distribution are ambiguous, because of the "dualism" that they risk creating within the economy. A high rate of unionization allows employees to protect wage levels relative to capital remuneration, but only in the sectors and businesses where unions are active. If higher wages lead to fewer jobs, the other side of a relative equalization of income within unionized sectors will be higher unemployment or lower wages in non-unionized sectors or a combination of both. The same is true with minimum wage laws. A higher minimum wage will increase wages at the low end of the scale, which will reduce wage inequality among employed workers, but also risks increasing unemployment and therefore income inequality in the population. Just how sizable this effect will be has been the subject of a great deal of controversy in the economic literature. In fact, the link between total employment and minimum wage appears to be rather limited in countries where the minimum wage is low relative to the whole wage scale. It is significantly negative in countries where the minimum wage has been set at a higher level, as in France where it stands at 60% of the median wage. Also, its effects often concentrate on certain categories of salaried employees, such as young people and women working part-time. In France, it is estimated that a 1% increase in the minimum wage would result in a 1% drop in employment of those working at this wage level (approximately 11% of the labor force), but possibly, through sub-

---

[16] See the numbers provided by the OECD: w://stats.oecd.org /Index.aspx?DataSetCode=RHMW.

stitution, would see an increase in jobs above the minimum wage depending on the degree of contagion of wage increases across wage levels. In the United States, this relationship is much weaker, principally because the minimum wage is itself much lower relative to the average or median salary of the workforce.[17]

At first glance, it may seem that the taxation and parafiscal taxation of wages to fund various forms of insurance, such as retirement or unemployment, as well as active labor market policies and professional training, would raise the cost of labor and would therefore have a negative effect on the volume of employment and an indirect negative effect on wages and income distribution. This is why we often hear that these need to be cut back. But it is not quite as simple as that. In the absence of a minimum wage, it is likely that over the long term it will be employees who end up paying these costs. Indeed, from the point of view of employers, what matters is the total cost of an employee and whether each individual's contribution to output is less than this cost. Since a cut in payroll charges or wage deductions does not necessarily modify the productivity of employees, a competitive labor market will adjust in such a way that the cost of labor for the employers is not modified. In such a competitive environment, all the adjustment will thus be on the net earnings of the employees. The effect on distribution then depends on the progressiveness,

[17] For France, see Francis Kramarz and Thomas Philipon, "The Impact of Differential Payroll Tax Subsidies on Minimum Wage Employment," *Journal of Public Economics* 82 (2001): 115–46. See also the synthesis of empirical studies by David Neumark and William Wascher, "Minimum Wages and Employment" (Institute for the Study of Labor, IZA Working Paper No. 2570, 2007).

regressiveness, or neutrality of these costs with respect to household income and the transfers they fund. The situation is different when minimum wage laws are in place, because then the costs cannot be passed on to employees at that wage level. In this situation, a reduction of costs will represent a lower cost of labor, and as a result a rise in the employment of unskilled labor.

Unemployment insurance is another commonly used instrument for regulating the labor market that has been under heavy pressure in several countries over the last two or three decades. The reasons for this are often budgetary, but they also stem from a desire to increase the incentives for households to find employment. A system of unemployment compensation that is overly generous in the length of time it can be claimed or percentage of wages it replaces is often believed to disincentivize people to seek new employment. While this is true, an overly strict system can prevent better matches between job seekers and employers and is therefore also inefficient.

Do the empirical studies on the comparative experiences of developed countries over the course of the last two or three decades provide us with a less ambiguous and clearer picture of the relationship between regulations of the labor market and inequality, one that could provide us with explanations for the general rise in inequalities over these years? In some cases the answer is yes, in others it is much more equivocal.

The diminished importance of unions and of centralized wage negotiations has contributed to rising inequality in several countries, both in wages and incomes. Several studies have reached this conclusion. In the case of the United States, David Card went so far as to estimate that the decline in unionization rates accounts for 15–20% of the rise in male wage inequality from 1973 to 1993.[18] An influential study of unemployment insurance arrived at the generally accepted conclusion that a reduction in the generosity of this insurance has had a positive impact on the employment rate, but an inegalitarian effect on income and even wages.[19] In other words, the loss of certain unemployment benefits has not been compensated by a surplus of employment opportunities.

The effect of a minimum wage on distribution is more ambiguous. Holding employment constant, a drop in minimum wages relative to the average wage or median wage will necessarily increase wage inequality. This effect will be accompanied by a positive impact on employment that increases the number of employees paid the minimum wage. This is indeed what several studies have found.[20] On the other hand, if we are interested in the standard of living

[18] David Card, "The Effect of Unions on Wage Inequality in the US Labor Market," *Industrial and Labor Relations Review* 54 (2001): 296–315. Using a different methodology, John di Nardo, Nicole Fortin, and Thomas Lemieux arrived at the same conclusion ("Labor Market Institutions and the Distribution of Wages, 1973–1992: A Semi-Parametric Approach," *Econometrica*, 64, no. 5 (1996): 1001–44). Looking at a cross-section of the OECD countries, the same type of result was found by Daniele Checchi and Cecilia Garcia-Penalosa, "Labour Market Institutions and Income Inequality," *Economic Policy*, 23, no. 56 (2008): 601–49, as well as by Winfried Koeninger, Marco Leonardi, and Luca Nunziata in "Labor Market Institutions and Wage Inequality," *Industrial and Labor Relations Review* 60, no. 3 (2007): 340–56.

[19] See Checchi and Garcia-Penalosa, "Labour Market Institutions," and Koeninger et al., "Labor Market Institutions and Wage Inequality."

[20] For the United States, see di Nardo et al., "Labor Market Institutions"; David Lee, "Wage Inequality in the United States during the 1980s: Rising Dispersion or Falling Minimum Wage?" *Quarterly Journal of Economics* 114, no. 3 (1999): 977–1023. For other countries, see Koeninger et al., "Labor Market Institutions and Wage Inequality."

distribution, we get different results. The effect that a change in the minimum wage will have on standard of living inequality will depend on the other sources of income available to the families that include members working at minimum wage. In fact, the effect is very limited. An econometric study conducted by Checchi and Garcia-Penalosa of a sample of sixteen developed countries between 1969 and 2004 concluded that there was no significant relationship between changes in minimum wage and the level of inequality in income distribution.[21]

The same conclusion holds when it comes to employment protection policies or payroll cost rates. Checchi and Garcia-Penalosa's study also found that they had no significant effect on income inequality, while, in its most recent report on inequality, the OECD found that stronger employment protection laws led to a less disparate wage distribution.[22] These results are not necessarily contradictory as they do not refer to the same concept of inequality: household income or standard of living inequality in the former case, and individual earnings inequality in the latter. Similar results are obtained with regard to an increase in payroll costs. I should also emphasize that these two types of policies tend to have a significant and positive effect on the unemployment rate.

[21] Checchi and Garcia-Penalosa, "Labour Market Institutions." Other studies based on a simple simulation of a rise in minimum wages over a sample of households do not necessarily arrive at the same result (see, for example, Stephen Machin and Alan Manning, "Minimum Wages and Economic Outcomes in Europe," *European Economic Review* 41, nos. 3–5 (2007): 733–42). But, of course, these omit the indirect employment effects that are implicitly taken into account by econometric analysis.

[22] OECD, *Divided We Stand: Why Inequality Keeps Rising* (Paris: OECD, 2011).

In summation, we have the empirical evidence to show, sometimes quite dramatically, that several features of the deregulation of the labor market have contributed to a rise in wage inequality and, in certain cases, to a rise in standard of living inequality as well. We also know that a great number of developed countries have liberalized their labor markets. Does this mean that we can determine how important a role these reforms have played in increasing inequality? In some countries, studies are available that can give us an idea. For instance, the drop in real minimum wage in the 1980s and 1990s and the weakening of the power of unions have been shown to be responsible for 20–30% of the increase in wage inequality in the United States. Analogous phenomena have taken place in other countries, but we have neither data nor the studies necessary to quantify them with any precision. In other cases, the inegalitarian effects of deregulation of the labor market were partially or even completely compensated for by other reforms of the labor market. For example, the effects of Denmark weakening its system of employment protection were balanced out by reforms that increased the efficiency of unemployment insurance and the system for retraining and reskilling the unemployed. There are other phenomena that can compensate for the weakening of one or more employment protection policies. But the important point here is that, all else being equal, the liberalization of the labor market that has taken place over the last three decades in a large number of developed countries will have contributed to the rise in wage inequality and, with certain specific types of reforms, income inequality as well. It is also possible that these measures contributed to an increase in the volume of jobs, but at the same time were responsible for increasing the job insecurity of certain sections of the labor force, via the mechanisms described previously.

Emerging Economies and Structural Adjustment

The preceding discussion focuses on developed countries. But emerging and developing economies have also undergone important reforms to their economic institutions, which were often imposed from the outside, notably in the context of the "structural adjustment" policies required by international financial institutions (the IMF and the World Bank) in the aftermath of the debt crisis of the 1980s. These structural adjustment policies have often been criticized for their social costs, partly because they slowed growth and thus the reduction of poverty dramatically, and partly because they placed more of the brunt of the costs of these programs on the lower and middle classes, rather than on the high end of the income scale.[23]

The debt crisis began in Latin America, specifically in Mexico in 1982, and for a decade and a half it would have harsh consequences for the developing world, in particular in sub-Saharan Africa and Latin America. The structural adjustment programs that the international financial institutions demanded in exchange for aid were grounded on a package of free market principles that were later baptized the "Washington consensus." They resulted in deep institutional changes: commercial and financial liberalization, deregulation of goods, capital and labor markets, privatization, the elimination of consumer and producer subsidies,

[23] See IMF-IEO, *Fiscal Adjustment in IMF-Supported Programs*, IMF, June 2002.

cuts in social spending, and so forth. As we have seen, many of these reforms almost certainly had inegalitarian effects, and, in fact, between the 1980s and 1990s we can see a substantial rise in inequalities in the countries affected most directly by these programs: Argentina, Mexico, Peru, Ecuador, and even Brazil. But it would be an error to attribute this entirely to the structural adjustment programs.

Latin America was in a difficult economic situation, one in need of radical reform. It is likely that inequality would have worsened no matter what these reforms were. In several cases, inequality had already begun to increase at the first signs of the crisis, when the rich began transferring their assets overseas to avoid the fallout. The example of the 2001 crisis in Argentina is instructive in this regard. Having turned down IMF intervention and decided to default on its debt, Argentina handled its crisis completely autonomously. After three years that were especially hard on the population, growth returned and remained at high levels. However, inequality had shot up in the adjustment process. The Gini coefficient, which was 0.50 in 1999, had risen to 0.54 in 2003 at the moment when the crisis was on the verge of turning back. It has since gone back down.

While this is true, there is little doubt that several structural reforms typical of the Washington consensus, in contrast to policies focused more directly on reestablishing macroeconomic equilibrium, such as those used by the Argentine government in response to the 2001 crisis (devaluation, disinflation, budgetary tightening), have had an inegalitarian effect on certain countries. This is certainly the case for policies like the elimination of input and output price subsidies for small farmers, the abandoning of consumer price subsidies, the rise in prices for certain privatized services, and, after some time delay, the cuts in public social spending on education and health. The transformation of public monopolies into poorly regulated private monopolies also allowed for the creation of new rents and sometimes even the accumulation of immense fortunes. The best example of this is Carlos Slim, who took advantage of the privatization of Mexican telecommunication companies to become the second richest man in the world.

Of course, these structural measures were often justified on grounds of economic efficiency. Quite apart from the fact that these reforms were frequently applied indiscriminately, they were also imposed abruptly at times and without much concern for equality and even less with protecting the poor. At the same time, the distributive effects of these policies were often perceived negatively, and it is possible that these policies have been blamed for an increase in inequality that was actually the result of the crisis itself and the macroeconomic policies necessary for reestablishing equilibrium. Looking at the inequality numbers does in fact show that they rose rapidly with the advent of the crisis and remained at high levels for as long as the economies in question had not returned to regular growth, which is to say, as long as the adjustments were not fully implemented.

Structural adjustment programs were also imposed on other countries in other continents. In Asia, inequality varied little. It even dropped in countries like Indonesia (before jumping back in the 1990s) or Pakistan, while it increased slightly in the Philippines. On the other hand, contrary to what happened in Latin America, structural adjustment in Asia allowed for a faster return to earlier levels of growth. In African countries, which were less developed and often endowed with a significant non-market sector, inequality was less sensitive to the reforms that came as pre-conditions on aid from development agencies. This does not mean that Africa did not suffer from the market liberalization measures imposed in conjunction with bailouts, or that these programs left the income distribution unchanged. In fact, African growth was seriously slowed, even reversed, in the 1980s, possibly because of the adjustment but also because of unfavorable terms of trade. The problem is that we do not track the evolution of distribution in this part of the world with the precision necessary for a detailed analysis.

Even if they also underwent wide-scale institutional changes under their own direction, the big Asian economies differ considerably from the above examples. For China, these institutional changes represented above all a transition from a centrally planned economy toward a market economy, rather than the modification of the functioning of some markets, as important as this may be. The liberation of individual initiative where before there had been little or none could only increase inequality. To a lesser extent, this applies to India as well, since it too was initially overregulated. Yet, in both cases, it is difficult to disentangle what part of the observed increase in inequality is due *stricto sensu* to the freeing of market forces, what part to the opening up to international trade and foreign investments, and what part as the direct consequences of the development process. What's more, we can observe that the rise in inequality at the moment of Eastern Europe's transition to a market economy was, in several countries, only temporary. Inequality fell once the economy had fully settled into the new regime and the mechanisms for redistributing income had been reconfigured. We don't observe such a turnaround among the Asian giants.

Globalization, Deregulation, Inequality

Around sixty years ago, the U.S. economist Simon Kuznets, who had studied the evolution of inequality in several developed countries, formulated a hypothesis that would become widely influential. His idea was that in an initial stage, the process of economic development increases inequality by displacing a portion of the population from traditional occupations toward more productive, but also more heterogeneous, jobs, thus creating more inequality. In a second stage, this trend in inequality reverses itself once the traditional sector has become a minority of the economy. In other words, over the course of the process of economic development, inequality follows an upside-down or inverted U-shaped curve.

The recent evolution in inequality within developed countries contradicts Kuznets's hypothesis. Inequality did indeed follow an inverted U curve until the middle of the 1970s. Since then, many developed nations have been adding a rising tail to the end of the inverted U, as inequality has been increasing once again. It may be that the rise in inequality we can observe in some emerging economies is obeying the same mechanism that Kuznets identified. The development of big industrial or urban centers where income is higher than in the traditional rural zones might explain growing inequality in China and India. But it would only be one explanation among many. Whichever economy we examine, the case seems clear: standard of living inequality is not governed by an iron law that ties it exclusively to its stage of economic development.

My examination of the variation in economic inequality within countries shows a complex evolution that is as much the product of more or less exogenous global economic phenomena (the expansion of international trade, or technological progress) as it is of the economic policies or the institutional reforms specific to a given country. There are various factors at play in the rise in inequality within countries: increased returns on physical, financial, and human (which is to say, of skilled labor) capital, economic restructuring, technological innovation, macroeconomic policy, taxation, and market deregulation, including the deregulation of the financial and labor markets. In a majority of countries, the conjunction of these effects has resulted in a significant rise in wage and income inequality. In others, economic policy or other endogenous mechanisms have partially counteracted these inegalitarian pressures, or even managed to reverse them.

Outside of the inegalitarian forces analyzed in this chapter, there are other changes in economic structures and demographics that can have an effect on inequality levels in a country, both positively and negatively. I have already discussed the way in which economic development can create more inequality before bringing it back down as the modern high-productivity sector expands and the traditional low-income sector shrinks. There are also the effects of changing demographics: declining birth rates can improve the standard of living of the poorest members of the population; a rise in the number of single-parent households or an increase in female labor force participation can substantially modify the distribution of household monetary standards of living in opposite directions; and by pairing people of comparable potential incomes together, a rise in endogamy may contribute to a rise in inequality. The reason that I have not emphasized these dynamics is that they seem relatively independent of globalization and are more country-specific than those forces that could potentially affect national inequality levels in general.

The wide range of factors has meant that there is a great deal of diversity when it comes to national experiences, with a majority of developed countries seeing a significant rise in inequality, while in others the rise has been moderate, or even nonexistent. We can observe this same diversity among emerging economies, which are also subject to the same global forces.

This analysis of the development of inequality within nations and its possible causes leads us to two conclusions. First of all, we should emphasize the major role played by globalization. It is the background for almost all that has happened. It has changed the international climate for all national economies and has profoundly modified their structures. By intensifying competition, it has accelerated the pace of technological innovation and its consequences. It has induced financial liberalization in a large number of countries and reinforced the mobility of capital. Although they are not presented as such here, the general deregulatory movement and the weakening of the progressiveness of taxation may themselves be an indirect consequence of globalization. Indeed, it has often been the case, especially over the more recent period, that these reforms were advocated as necessary to maintain national competitiveness and the capacity for innovation in the face of rising international competition. Through these different channels, globalization may have thus managed to have a major impact on the distribution of income, even if other factors, specific to different countries, have sometimes either exacerbated its effects or canceled them out.

The second conclusion is that we should emphasize the role and importance of economic policies. These policies are generally justified in the name of two very different principles: efficiency and/or equality. Over the last few decades, it would seem as if the first principle has generally won out over the latter. In the name of economic efficiency, a number of reforms have been undertaken that were intended to improve the competitiveness of national economies, notably, as argued earlier, in the face of the disequilibria caused by globalization. But these very reforms have often contributed to a rise in inequality, without necessarily having had a major effect on efficiency.

We must therefore examine policies that target inequality more directly, and ask whether there are policies that could simultaneously serve to promote equality and efficiency, at both the national and international levels. This will be the task of the following chapters.

CHAPTER 4

Toward a Fair Globalization: Prospects and Principles

Globalization has played a significant role in the evolution of inequality in the world. It has made it possible for inequality to decrease between countries, pulling several hundred million people above the threshold of absolute poverty. On the other hand, within nations globalization has often directly or indirectly contributed to a rise in inequality. Directly, because it has lowered the relative compensation for unskilled labor in developed countries which face direct competition from the cheap labor costs of emerging economies, and also because it has increased the profits and remuneration of capital and highly skilled labor across the world. Indirectly, through the deep structural changes produced by the heightened competition between and within nations. In short, it may be the case that globalization is shifting global inequality from inequality across countries to inequality within a number of countries, in particular advanced countries but also several major emerging countries. Of course, other phenomena have contributed to this growth of inequality within countries, ranging from technological progress to the expansion of the financial sector to a doctrinal shift in favor of free market economics. But these phenomena themselves are not entirely independent of globalization and the competition it has triggered.

Even if we recognize the relationship between globalization and increases in inequality within a number of countries, we should not take it as a fait accompli. If we think that excessive levels of inequality within a nation are morally unacceptable, economically costly, and socially dangerous, then we should seek to identify and implement policies that would permit us to correct these inequalities or prevent them from emerging, while allowing the economic forces contributing to the reduction of inequality between countries to continue to develop.

In this chapter and the next I aim to answer three sets of questions. The first set concerns the middle and long-term future. Will the trends in global inequality that we've identified persist over the coming years, or will they fade? The second set of questions looks at whether we should adopt a laissez-faire approach. Inequality between countries has decreased and this is a good thing, but within a large number of economies it has risen to levels that are becoming worrisome. Is internal inequality the price that we must pay for the efficient development of national economies in a globalized world? What do basic economic theories tell us about the existence or the nonexistence of such a trade-off?

The third set of questions is the most important and the most complex of the three. It is concerned with identifying those policies that most effectively control increases in national inequality at the same time as maintaining economic efficiency in both the global and the national economies. This will be the subject of the next and last chapter of this book.

The Future of Inequality between Countries

Economic forecasting is always a delicate matter, especially when the world economy is just beginning to emerge—although this itself is uncertain—from an economic crisis of a severity it has not seen in a very long time. We can be almost certain, however, that developed countries will continue to grow more slowly than the big emerging economies, especially those in Asia, as has been the case over the last two or three decades. Located at the technological frontier of their production potential, developed countries have, as a group, grown at a rate largely determined by the advance of technological progress as it advances upon this frontier, or a 2–3% growth per year in the most dynamic countries and 1–2% in the others. The emerging economies, on the other hand, are still far from this frontier, and their growth is therefore not limited to the same extent by technological constraints. Instead, it will depend above all on their capacity for human, organizational, and material investment and their ability to adapt imported modes of production and management to their own specific environment and the extent to which their economic and political institutions are able to evolve in a way that effectively supports development.[1]

The gap in productivity between developed economies and emerging economies is still wide enough for the process of catching up to last for a long time. Taking into account a gradual deceleration in growth rates over the long term, it will take a good three decades for Chinese income per capita to reach the standard of living that we observe today in the least rich OECD countries. Of course, events might occur along the way that would draw out this process, and it is even conceivable that China will never fully catch up. However, it remains unlikely that the convergence between emerging and developed economies will cease over the medium term.

There are two additional reasons to support this prognosis. The first concerns the medium term and the second, the long term. The crisis from which developed economies are beginning to emerge will have lasting effects. Even if it were possible to avert a new financial crisis or a new recession in the years to come, which is not certain, growth in these economies will remain constrained by debt reduction and, more important, by structural changes imposed by the continuing slow process of deindustrialization. Some economists also predict a slowing down in the rate of technological progress which they believe may last for some time.[2] On the other hand, even if some of them are partially affected by the slowed growth of rich countries, the emerging economies often have large domestic markets that offer

[1] Acemoglu et al., "Distance to Frontier, Selection, and Economic Growth."

[2] See, for instance, Robert Gordon, "Is US Economic Growth Over? Faltering Innovation Confronts the Six Headwinds," Working Paper 18315, National Bureau of Economic Research, Cambridge, MA, 2012.

substantial and autonomous opportunities for growth. China's current attempt to reorient its development toward domestic demand is a good example of this. In addition, the rapid development of South-South trade could, with some adjustments, be a substitute for the role played by demand from developed countries. It is therefore likely that the longer it takes the developed world to fully recover from the present crisis, the faster the convergence between emerging and developed economies will be.

Over the longer term, we must hope that the global community will finally decide to engage seriously in the struggle against climate change. If this is the case, it is also likely that the agreement they would settle on would place higher costs on richer countries than on developing ones, without necessarily diminishing the gap in growth rates, and therefore without hampering the ability of developing countries to catch up.

From the perspective of the global standard of living distribution, an important implication of this catching-up process is worth emphasizing. After a certain point, the faster development of emerging economies relative to both developed economies and the global average is likely to increase rather than diminish global inequality. China is the clearest example of this. When the average Chinese standard of living will be somewhat above the world average, any additional growth in China in relation to the rest of the world will become a potential source of increasing global inequality, because, roughly speaking, it would be contributing to the relative enrichment of a country whose standard of living is in the upper part of the global distribution. With the present growth trends in the world, simple calculations based on the data used in chapter 1 suggest that this will take less than twenty years and that faster growth in China will have increasingly less impact on levels of global inequality.

Making Sub-Saharan Africa "Emerge"

The economic outlook for poor countries over the medium- and long-term seems more uncertain than it is for the emerging economies. While it is true that sub-Saharan Africa's growth has accelerated over the last several years, the causes of this acceleration are far from clear. Some think that this is the result of an improvement in economic and political governance, specifically in more rigorous macroeconomic management. Others argue that it is due above all to an improvement in the terms of trade, to the rising prices of natural resources and primary agricultural commodities and, in several countries, the beginning of the extraction of recently discovered resource deposits. Even if it is difficult to generalize, there are several factors that favor the second interpretation.

If this analysis is correct, the big question is whether raw material prices will remain at their current relative levels in the years to come, or whether they will drop back down. In any event, the important point is that, unlike the emerging economies, it is not clear that poor countries have embarked on an autonomous process of catching up with the more advanced countries. Prior to the 2008 crisis and over the last few years, they benefited from an extremely favorable global economic climate, but it is uncertain whether this situation will persist. In particular, it is somewhat worrisome to observe that, despite the clear acceleration of growth over the last ten to fifteen years, no noticeable structural change is taking place in African economies. It is as if most of this growth was essentially driven by the additional demand arising from favorable terms of trade: on average in the region, the GDP share of both manufacturing and agriculture keeps going down whereas that of construction, services, or trade is going up.

Over time, it is the growth performances of these countries that will determine whether or not global inequality between countries will continue its historic decline. Because these are the poorest countries on the planet, and at the same time the countries with the highest rates of demographic growth, their economic performance will also determine the evolution of world poverty.

We saw in chapter 1 that several poor countries in sub-Saharan Africa had "decoupled" relative to the rest of the world over the period from 1989 to 2008. In most cases, political difficulties can explain this decoupling. During the 1980s and the first half of the 1990s, it was the region as a whole, and not a few countries, that fell increasingly far behind the rest of the world, both for reasons of political instability as well as an unfavorable global economic climate. We must prevent this situation from repeating itself if we wish to see the decline in global standard of living inequality persist. The goal now is no more and no less than that of making poor sub-Saharan African countries, and the poor countries of the world in general, "emerge." This is all the more important given that the relative demographic weight of the region is bound to increase very significantly in the coming decades. Current projections predict the sub-Saharan African population to double by 2050, to make up more than 20% of the world population.

Inequality within Countries

Predicting what will happen in the future is even more tricky when it comes to inequality within countries. One reason for this is the important role of inequality-correcting policies and institutional reforms. These can work in completely opposite ways, either canceling out or even reversing the effects of market forces or accentuating the effects of those forces working in favor of greater equality. Another reason it is difficult to make predictions is the heterogeneity of countries. Nonetheless, we can look at recent developments and attempt to extrapolate certain trends that would be compatible with a plausible scenario for the global economy.

Will the slowed global growth that we can expect to result from the adjustments currently taking place in a large number of developed economies temper the pace of globalization and its effects on distribution in national economies? It is not clear. Certainly we might think that because globalization involves an increase in the external trade of all countries, decreasing the imports of some would slow the development of exports in others. But the important point is that the process of globalization largely affects the fundamental restructuring of the global apparatus of production, in particular the increasing international fragmentation of the "value chain," which is to say the sequence of operations that leads to a final product. This fragmentation is itself the result of the central role played by the development strategies of companies, which are becoming increasingly multinational and whose production operations are now being planned and managed at a global level.

It is unclear whether slowing global demand, tied to the pressures on developed economies and the reorientation of certain emerging economies toward their domestic markets, will significantly affect this restructuring. On the contrary, this crisis could even accelerate this trend, in the likely event that the big multinational companies attempt to compensate for the weakening of a portion of their demand by reducing their cost and increasing their productivity through deeper globalization of their activity and possibly an acceleration of their technological development.

Another factor that could lead to more inequality in advanced countries may be the continuing increase of the wealth/income ratio emphasized by Piketty. As seen in the preceding chapter, his argument is that this is due to the slowing down in the long-run growth rate of developed economies, which have not yet reached the steady state associated with this lower rate. The convergence of this kind of process, essentially based on wealth accumulation behavior, is extremely slow. On the other hand, globalization tends to equalize the rate of return on wealth across countries, thus preventing it from falling in advanced countries as the result of more wealth becoming available per capita. For these two reasons, an increase in the capital share in national income and therefore in income inequality in those countries still seems unavoidable for some time.[3]

At the end of the day, barring some catastrophic event that overturns the world economy as it works today, the forces of globalization and technological innovation, which have had such a strong influence on the distribution

[3] Note that this argument would apply even without any increase in the inequality of the wealth distribution, a rather controversial issue in Piketty's recent book.

of income within nations over the course of the last three decades, are likely to continue to have an effect in the future, although it remains uncertain just how strong that influence will be. Thus, when it comes to the distribution of income in developed economies, the pressure in favor of capital and highly skilled labor will continue, to the detriment of low- and even medium-skilled workers. The forces in favor of inequality will remain in place, while the restructuring of economic sectors will lead to an increased precariousness in the labor market. The outlook is troubling unless we can find a way to manage these forces and neutralize their effects.

In the emerging economies, growth that remains fast-paced and, perhaps, a greater focus on internal markets will permit the integration of the rural masses into the modern sector of the economy, contributing to a reduction in poverty and certain equalization of income, following the Kuznets model mentioned in the previous chapter. Nonetheless, the same inegalitarian pressures in favor of capital and the highly skilled should also be observable.

Ultimately, putting aside policies that correct for inequality, the slow and still partial equalization of the price of factors of production that seems to have been taking place across the world over the last two or three decades, should continue to influence the distribution of standard of living in most national economies.

Yet, the situation of poor countries, principally in sub-Saharan Africa, could be different. A distinction should be made between the countries whose recent growth rests first and foremost on the exploitation of natural resources, which currently fetch high prices on international markets, and those whose reforms have brought them closer to the point where they could reach economic "takeoff." For the first group, there is a high risk that the revenues from natural resources (oil, mineral, agricultural products) are being monopolized by a small section of society with little benefit to the rest of the population. This is already the case in a large number of countries. We can thus imagine that rapid GDP growth will be accompanied by a rise in true, as opposed to observed,[4] inequality and a slow reduction of poverty—perhaps even a rise due to demographic pressure.

The future will be different for countries where reforms, notably in governance, permit a more transparent management of resources. But even in these countries, there is reason to doubt that growth on the "emirates" model, which is to say, based exclusively on rents from natural resources and on meeting the resulting demand for nontradable goods and services, is possible over the long term, given the size of these countries and their rates of demographic growth. Is it really possible to imagine that Nigeria (150 million inhabitants today and a projected 280 million by 2050) or the Democratic Republic of Congo (70 million today, a projected 180 million in 2050) could follow the model of rentier development of Dubai or Abu Dhabi (around 1.5–2 million inhabitants each, but only 500,000 of whom are nationals and three times that number of immigrants)? Could these big African countries bypass development based on either industrialization or gains in agricultural productivity, which characterized other emerging economies endowed with significant natural resource wealth (Brazil, Indonesia, Malaysia)?

[4] As mentioned in chapter 1, inequality estimated from household surveys in developing countries rather generally miss the top incomes and the economic and political elites. To a larger extent than in developed countries, they thus underestimate the true level of inequality.

In sum, there are two main forces that seem capable of affecting global inequality in the future: the potential for growth in emerging countries and the process of globalization. The first should allow emerging countries to continue to catch up with rich countries, independently of the processes of globalization itself and the existing global economic climate (to the extent that emerging countries can rely on their internal markets and South-South commerce). Yet, this positive outlook for inequality between countries has to be tempered by the uncertainty surrounding the poor countries that are mainly natural resource or primary agricultural commodity exporters. In relation to inequality within nations, however, the process of globalization is likely to remain the dominant force. If this process continues and deepens, it will prolong the rise in inequalities within developed countries and in certain developing countries. For the latter, the equalizing effects of economic development might temper the trend toward inequality. But this trend could actually be exacerbated in poor countries whose development is based primarily on exporting natural resources. Overall, it seems likely that the trend toward inequality between countries being replaced by inequality within countries at the global level might still be present in the decades to come.

Of course, this does not account for the effect that other major trends or events could have on the global and the national economies, such as for instance global warming, the collapse of the euro zone, conflict in the Middle East, a difficult democratic transition in China. In my discussion so far I have also set aside national redistribution policies that could contain or even reduce inequalities within a country. But do these measures actually work and do they not also carry the risk of stifling a country's potential for economic growth? The underlying hypothesis of the prospective analysis given previously is that, in the world as in countries, things are evolving under laissez faire—as is often advocated by those who argue that correcting for inequalities would necessarily entail a loss of economic efficiency. But is it correct, or even economically justified, to adopt this attitude?

Must We Choose between Equality and Economic Efficiency?

The debate in economics over the question of what relationship exists between inequality and economic efficiency has a long history. It is the source of intense disagreements that have sometimes taken on doctrinal dimensions. It is important to understand the elements of this debate, so that we can make an informed assessment of the policies that should be implemented in order to control inequality at the lowest cost to the economy.

A central tenet of economic theory is that the redistribution of income cannot be lump sum, because redistribution instruments—that is, taxes and transfers of all types— are based on the income economic agents generate through their activity and how they spend it. Under these conditions, income and wealth redistribution policies will necessarily distort the operation of markets and make the economy inefficient in the sense that it will no longer operate at maximum capacity on its production frontier. Therefore, there will inevitably be trade-offs between equality and efficiency. In other words, the simple fact of dividing the cake more equally will shrink the size of the cake, because it will distort the behavior of agents and the operation of mar

kets. Taxing the income that an individual gains from his
or her economic activity will reduce the incentive to work,
start a business, or invest. Distributing revenue from taxation to the rest of the population could have negative consequences on the supply of labor. The result would be a
lower volume of goods and services available in the economy, and therefore a drop in efficiency.[5]

Given how fundamental this theory is to basic economic
thinking, it is not surprising that it plays a central role in
debates over inequality and the methods for correcting it.
However, outside of the restrictive theoretical framework
of an economy in which all markets are perfectly competitive, the hypothesis that there is an inverse relationship between efficiency and equality is not very robust. In fact the
more important question would seem to be whether, starting from an initial position that is inefficient because of
certain market imperfections, there might be another situation, one that could be brought about through state intervention, that would improve total income and would at the
same time be more equal.

It does seem that some policies that aim to redistribute
income to the underprivileged also reduce the total income
of the population as a whole and are therefore economically inefficient. Imposing a marginal tax rate of 90% on all
income above a certain threshold would, if this threshold
was set low enough, end up stifling an economy's ability to

---

[5] Note that the concept of efficiency used here is that of "aggregate" efficiency rather than the Pareto efficiency familiar to economists, according
to which a situation is efficient if no agent can be made better off without
another one being made worse off. In the absence of lump-sum transfers,
there also is a trade-off between equality and Pareto efficiency. As the argument is a bit more technical, however, we stick to the simpler concept of
aggregate efficiency in what follows.

grow. Similarly, guaranteeing every citizen a relatively high minimum income without any counterbalances would inevitably reduce the total supply of labor in the economy. Fortunately, however, there are policies that both redistribute income, or modify the distribution of production factors, and improve the overall efficiency of the economy, especially given that inequality itself can have a negative effect on economic efficiency.

The Negative Consequences of Inequality

Over the last two decades, both theoretical and empirical economists have put a great deal of effort into trying to better understand the relationship between equality and efficiency and demonstrating ways that they can be complementary when they are too often seen as conflicting. There are several reasons that excessive rates of inequality could present a hindrance to the functioning of the economy. I will look at two of the main groups of arguments, the first of which focuses on market imperfections and the second on the effect that inequality can have on the social and political stability of a society, as well as on its governance. I will then briefly examine some of the empirical evidence for these different hypotheses.

Credit market imperfections are probably the most basic example of the way in which equality and efficiency can be complementary. We know that in any economy it can be difficult to obtain a bank loan without offering a guarantee, such as real estate property or financial wealth, or relying on parents or friends who agree to act as co-signers. Therefore, a potential entrepreneur who has no wealth and no network of connections will often have to give up on a brilliant idea that would have created jobs and value, simply because he lacks the necessary collateral or guarantee. On the other hand, a different entrepreneur who has access to capital or to good connections will be able to create a business that is less commercially or socially valuable than the first one would have been. Thus, inequality in wealth or connections, which leads to inequality in access to credit, is clearly a source of inefficiency. If we had to choose just one of these projects to come to fruition, society would choose the first one. However, it is the second one that we will end up with. Not only does inequality of access to credit create economic inefficiency; it also generates market income inequality since the first potential entrepreneur ends up less well off than the second.

Similar situations are also far too common with regard to education. Talented students may not have access to higher education, either because their parents do not have sufficient means to fund them or because the system of student loans has gaps, or because the environment they grew up in did not encourage them to prioritize their academic studies. On the other hand, students born into wealthier families are able to go to college even though they are less talented and society will benefit less from their education.

We could list many other examples of this type, some of which are more relevant to developing countries and others to more developed economies: landowners who let their land sit fallow while farm laborers have no land to work, buildings left vacant by their owners while there are homeless people, children from poor neighborhoods with little hope or expectations from life, racial and gender discrimination in the marketplace, and so on. In all of these cases, market imperfections are responsible for unequal access to crucial services or supplies, resulting in the failure of opportunities and potential to be exploited, while other less promising opportunities are fulfilled.

These inequalities, connected to the poor functioning of markets, are linked to the concept of inequality of opportunities discussed chapter 2. Because they precede the process of income formation, they may explain both income inequality and economic inefficiency. They also illustrate why interventions intended to increase equality of opportunity are likely to have positive impacts on both income distribution and economic efficiency in general.

The second channel through which inequality can have undesirable effects on economic efficiency is through the "spontaneous" redistribution that it can engender through various social and political mechanisms. A good example of this is the cost of the endemic violence afflicting certain countries or cities. Without any hope of ever joining the middle class, some youth in Brazilian *favelas*, Colombian *poblaciones*, and even the poor neighborhoods or *banlieues* of certain large cities in developed countries will try to make money from criminal activity: theft, assault, kidnapping, drug trafficking. The rest of the population is then obliged to allocate a significant part of their income to security in order to protect themselves. Anyone who has walked through Rio, Bogotá, or Mexico City will have been struck by the walls, bars, and security personnel—often heavily armed—that guard apartment buildings, stores, banks, and company headquarters. A few years ago, it was estimated that 10% of the labor force in Bogotá was employed in the security sector. Does this sound like an "efficient" situation? Wouldn't it be better if the same volume of labor—although not necessarily the same people—were allocated to the production of public and private goods or services?

And wouldn't it be easier, in order to achieve this goal, to reduce the inequality that leads to this criminality?

In fact, statistical studies showing a relationship between income inequality and criminality are not always convincing.[6] The problem is that it is not clear which dimension of inequality is relevant. Is it the gap between the very rich and the very poor, or the gap between the middle class and the poor? Is it a question of income inequality, monetary poverty, or inequality of opportunity (a concept that is ill suited to statistical measurement)?

More generally, whatever society we are talking about, it is reasonable to imagine that a substantial rise in inequality, or even the perception of a rise above a certain threshold, will inevitably lead to societal tension and political instability, both of which are detrimental to economic activity. Extreme cases of this would be the civil conflicts or large-scale revolutionary movements that, throughout history, have almost always incorporated claims about certain types of inequality. When it comes to the contemporary era, Alberto Alesina and Roberto Perotti have shown that political instability in developing economies, as represented by an indicator that takes into account attempted coups d'état and assassinations as well as the number of casualties in domestic conflicts, can be at least partially explained by the degree of inequality in a given country, and has, unsurprisingly, a negative effect on investment and growth.[7]

---

[6] This is because of the essentially cross-country nature of exising evidence. See, for instance, Daniel Lederman, Norman Loayza, and Pablo Fajnzylber, "What Causes Violent Crime?" *European Economic Review* 46 (2002): 1323–57.

[7] Alberto Alesina and Roberto Perotti, "Income Distribution, Political Instability and Investment," *European Economic Review* 40, no. 6 (1996): 1203–28.

This kind of violence is obviously rare in democratic societies. But they are not immune to social movements of varying sizes rooted in rising inequality or, at the very least, the feeling among a segment of the population that such an increase has occurred. Examples of this in the recent crisis include the demonstrations against austerity in Greece, the *indignados* movement in Spain, and, of course, "Occupy Wall Street" in the United States. In one way or another, all of these movements criticized excessive inequality—e.g., the "top 1%"—and the very unequal impact of the crisis on different sectors of society.

In democratic countries, the conflict over distribution can be managed more directly through the system of taxation and transfers, but even this approach can have a negative impact on economic efficiency. For example, a democratic society in which markets have created a very unequal income distribution is likely to be a society in which a majority of citizens will be in favor of sharp redistribution. But if this redistribution results in market distortions and economic inefficiency, as economic theory suggests, then we could say that the initial levels of inequality (in primary income prior to taxes and transfers) created inefficiency. If there is too much inequality starting out, then a majority of citizens might demand more redistribution, which in turn can lead to a less efficient economy or slower growth, by discouraging investment and entrepreneurship through excessive taxation on income, for example.[8]

---

[8] This argument was first developed by Alberto Alesina and Dani Rodrik, "Distributive Politics and Economic Growth," *Quarterly Journal of Economics* 109, no. 2 (1994): 465–90; and Torsten Persson and Guido Tabellini, "Is Inequality Harmful for Growth?" *American Economic Review* 84, no. 3 (1994): 600–621.

However, this argument is not always convincing. Even in a democratic society, high levels of inequality can result in more power being concentrated in the hands of an economic elite, given that they have more means at their disposal to lobby the government and influence the way people vote. In such a situation, redistribution can be limited, even nonexistent. In certain cases, redistribution can even switch directions, with money flowing from the working and middle classes to the very rich, not necessarily through regressive taxes and transfers but because the elite are able to acquire monopoly power in some key sectors of the economy. This is what we see in undemocratic democratic societies where high levels of inequality go hand in hand with mediocre governance or regulation and are extremely unfavorable to development.[9]

The recent debate over the hypothesis that the financial and economic crisis in the United States was in part the result of rising inequalities offers a good illustration of several of the arguments presented here.[10] According to this hypothesis, we might have expected that the transfer of income from the low end of the distribution to the high end

[9] On the influence of inequality on political power in the United States, see Martin Gilens, *Affluence and Influence: Economic Inequality and Political Power in America* (Princeton, NJ: Princeton University Press, 2013). For the role of governance in development, see Daron Acemoglu and James Robinson, *Why Nations Fail: The Origin of Power, Prosperity and Poverty* (New York: Crown Business, 2012).

[10] This hypothesis, often attributed to Joseph Stiglitz, *The Price of Inequality*, has been the focus of several analyses. See, for example, Michael Kumhof and Romain Rancière, "Inequality, Leverage and Crises," IMF Working Paper, no. 10/268, 2011). For a critique of this hypothesis, see Edward Glaeser, "Does Economic Inequality Cause Crises?", *New York Times*, Economix Blog, 2010. A recent synthesis of the debate is put forward by Till van Treeck, "Did Inequality Cause the U.S. Financial Crisis?", *Journal of Economic Surveys*, 10.1111, 2013.

and the rising income inequality observed over the two or three decades before the crisis would be accompanied by a decrease in consumption and therefore a drop in economic activity. If this did not happen, it was because there was an expansion of credit, specifically mortgage lending, to lower income households, who had previously been excluded from this market. This expansion was financed in part by the extra income saved by the richest households and brought about by increasing inequality. In other words, two mechanisms, each of them involving a different kind of inequality, came into play, and, for a while at least, balanced each other out. On the one hand, more income flowed to the richest segment of society, and on the other, part of that income was redistributed to the poorer levels through more credit.

We know how this story ends. The increased demand for housing that resulted from the expansion of lending due to extra loanable funds, as well as the securitization of mortgage loans that was supposed to mutualize default risk on mortgage loans, fueled a bubble. In turn, this led to an increase in the consumption of households that, in the United States, could take out loans against the latent capital gains of their home. Stimulated by this consumption, the growth in production sped up, giving the illusion that the country had entered a new period of prosperity. But, as of 2006, the increased number of "at risk" borrowers on the mortgage market led to defaults on loans, and the vicious downward spiral began: banks began giving less credit, fewer houses were bought, prices sank, further insolvency resulted, more heavily indebted households defaulted, construction stopped, and so on.

Various explanations have been given for the expansion of credit to lower-income households that for a time compensated for the recessive effects of rising inequality and ended up triggering the financial crisis. According to Raghuram Rajan and to Joseph Stiglitz,[11] political concerns motivated some leaders to look for a way to compensate for the stagnation or excessively slow growth in the standards of living of a large percentage of the population relative to the most well-off. This is the same argument about endogenous redistribution caused by excessive inequality mentioned earlier and resulted from politicians pushing for the expansion of credit and involuntarily sparking the crisis by pushing easy lending as a remedy for rising inequality. Daron Acemoglu, on the other hand, argues that it was the economic elites who took advantage of the growing resources at their disposal to convince political leaders to reform the financial system, specifically with regard to mortgage loans, for their own advantage and without concern for collective risks.[12] Again, this is the equivalent of the argument outlined above of elite-capture caused by excessive inequality. For others, the expansion of credit essentially resulted from households trying to stop their consumption from falling behind the U.S. average and getting into debt as a result.

Of course, any or all of these hypotheses are part of an explanation of the crisis, but none of them fully explain it. While rising inequality may well have played an important role, the crisis itself was facilitated by other factors. Historically low interest rates caused by the flow of Asian capi-

---

[11] Raghuram G. Rajan, *Fault Lines: How Hidden Fractures Still Threaten the World Economy* (Princeton, NJ: Princeton University Press, 2010); Stiglitz, *The Price of Inequality.*

[12] Daron Acemoglu, "Thoughts on Inequality and the Financial Crisis," presentation at the American Economic Association, 2011; http://economics.mit.edu/files/6348.

tal into the United States, the loosening of monetary policy following the 9/11 attacks and the dot-com crisis of the early 2000s had lowered the cost of credit and led banks to lend more and therefore to take on more risk. In addition, we should not leave out a financial sector submerged in securitization, subprime mortgages, and credit default swaps,[13] which had significantly increased its systemic vulnerability.

Because of this, it will be some time before we can measure with precision the role rising inequality played in the crash. We can nonetheless surmise that the explosive rise in inequalities, which resulted in the slower growth, sometimes even stagnation, of real income for the majority of the American population, would not have been compatible with high levels of American economic growth without some motor pushing U.S. households to increase their consumption spending. Without more credit, the sluggishness of internal demand would have stifled growth for a certain period of time.

At a more general level, we must admit that it is extremely difficult to demonstrate empirically the consequences of excessive levels of inequality or that these would cause significant variations in a country's macroeconomic performance. Inequality is not exogenous. It is as much an influence on the economy as it is the result of it, which means that it is not an easy task to identify a clear causal relationship. Furthermore, we cannot always be certain that we are tracking the dimensions of inequality most likely to influence the behavior of economies. Which one would it be: inequality of income, opportunity, or wealth? Between the richest and the poorest? Between the rich and

---

[13] Instruments to insure against potential defaults by the borrowers.

the middle class? It's not surprising that in these conditions, cross-sectional analyses that compare the degree of inequality in different countries with various measurements of economic performance often end up with ambiguous results.

Conversely, at the microeconomic level we do have empirical evidence that amply demonstrates the existence of market imperfections and inequalities in access to services like credit, education, healthcare, and the legal system, inequalities that we know will result in income inequality and economic inefficiency, even if we cannot assess its impact at the aggregate level.

Before concluding this quick review of the negative consequences of inequality, a word must be said about the hypothesis that economic inequality may also have important indirect societal costs, independently of particular people seeing their income going up or down in comparison with others'. In particular, there is this hypothesis, popularized by Richard Wilkinson and Kate Pickett,[14] that income inequality could also have an adverse effect on people's health, quite independently from their income. If this were the case, it would probably be one of the most persuasive arguments against inequality. The reason I did not mention it, however, is that unfortunately the evidence to support that hypothesis is rather weak. There is indeed a relationship between income inequality and the mean health status of a population. But it could be due exclusively to the fact that on the one hand there is a correlation between individual health and income, and, on the other hand, it tends to disappear for high incomes. Thus, in one society

[14] A similar hypothesis is proposed in Richard Wilkinson and Kate Pickett, *The Spirit Level: Why Equality Is Better for Everyone* (New York: Penguin Books, 2009).

where rich people are richer and poor people poorer than in another society, rich people have the same health status but poor people are less healthy. On average, health is worse in the more unequal society. The same kind of correlation with income inequality may be observed for all types of behavior linked in some nonlinear way to income. We have seen this is the case for crime.

The Wilkinson hypothesis goes beyond such a correlation, however. In the case of health, all people in the more unequal society should report a lower health status, independent of their income. One possible explanation would be the stress arising from trying to climb the income ladder. More efforts are needed to pass each rung of the ladder in a more unequal society or to maintain oneself on the same rung. For this hypothesis to be validated, we should observe health to be affected by inequality after controlling for individual income. A lot of research has been done in this direction, but the evidence does not conform to that hypothesis.[15]

Although economic inequality does not seem to have an indirect societal effect on health, it remains the case that it may have sizable economic and social costs. Contrary to what is often said, inequality and economic performance are not independent of each other. We have seen that a rise in certain types of inequality can have negative effects on economic efficiency, and while these effects can be modest over a certain range of inequality levels, economic theory and several pieces of empirical evidence show that beyond a certain threshold they can become an obstacle or even a regressive force. It remains extremely difficult to put any

[15] Owen O'Donnell, Eddy Van Doorslaer, and Tom Van Ourti, "Health and Inequality," in Atkinson and Bourguignon, *Handbook of Income Distribution*, chapter 17, offer an exhaustive survey of all these issues.

kind of number on this threshold, which will moreover depend heavily on national contexts.

Given the uncertainty about these thresholds, fighting against rising inequality, which has followed long periods of stability, seems crucial not only from the point of view of social justice, but also as an essential safeguard for preserving societal stability and economic performance. Not doing so would be equivalent to gambling on the point at which more inequality may become a serious obstacle for economic progress or might even trigger social movements that may threaten the existing economic order. We do not know where this threshold lies, but we know there is such a threshold and that economic losses will appear well before it is reached. If there is any truth in the argument that the recent crisis is due to the high level of inequality reached in some advanced countries, we might already be observing this process at work.

Redistribution and Equality of Opportunity

There are three main points that we should take away from this discussion about the relationship between inequality and economic efficiency: (a) there is a danger that allowing inequalities to rise unhindered could result in an increasing loss of efficiency; (b) there can be significant drops in incentives and therefore in economic performance linked to correcting economic inequality through the redistribution of current income (i.e., taxes and transfers); and (c) reducing discrimination and exclusion of all kinds, in other words, leveling the field of equality of opportunity, could both reduce economic inequality and lead to gains in efficiency for the economy as whole. Given these conditions, shouldn't we focus primarily on overcoming discrimination, exclusion, and market failures such that all citizens can enjoy the same chances of obtaining, through talent, hard work, or entrepreneurship, a satisfactory standard of living? More equal opportunities and less primary income inequality would then allow economies to grow energetically and harmoniously. Or will we also need to resort to redistributing income through conventional means?

Actually, there is no simple answer, and we need to be able to equalize opportunities and to effect the redistribution of income. Making progress on equality of opportunity often requires additional investments in public services. For example, ensuring equal access to a quality education, in such a way as to optimize the abilities and talents of the population as a whole, requires increased state spending. This is true in developing countries, where the rates of secondary, and sometimes even primary, schooling remain very low. It is also true in developed countries, where education quality can vary widely. Moreover, covering these costs requires increased government revenue, generally coming from taxes. Whether these taxes are paid by all citizens in proportion to their income, or whether they are progressive and focus only on the highest incomes, in the end such a policy does constitute redistribution from the wealthiest to the worst off, who are initially disadvantaged in the area of education.

Is this redistribution economically efficient? To the extent that it requires increased tax pressure on incomes, it could lead to a distortion of incentives and could be inefficient over the short term. But to the extent that it equalizes the chances of developing the talents of all, it contributes to efficiency over the medium and long terms. What is the overall result? Our final evaluation of this policy must depend on a large number of parameters, including notably the time preference of society. All things being equal, leaders who place more importance on the long term will tend to implement this kind of redistribution. Leaders who are more shortsighted will probably reject it.

Yet, the same principles of long-term economic efficiency can also be invoked to justify more direct forms of redistribution. "Poverty traps" are a feature of many societies. Once people have fallen below a certain income threshold or have dropped out of the labor market, after a certain period of time we begin to see a marked decline in their productivity as well as in their ability to function normally in the economic system. Over time, these people find themselves increasingly excluded. Efficiency concerns would dictate that we should employ "social assistance" programs to transfer purchasing power to individuals confronted with these situations, whether it be because they lost their jobs, experienced health problems, or suffered family tragedies, in order to help them return to the labor market. At the same time, it is true that this type of insurance can also create a disincentive to work, which is why we must optimize these programs in such a way as to ensure that their net effect on economic efficiency is positive.

A final justification for income redistribution as a means to preserve efficiency over the long term comes from the inequality of opportunity that is created by the intergenerational transmission of wealth. The persistent rise in primary income inequality risks perpetuating itself through the accumulation of inherited wealth, reinforcing asymmetries of opportunity in the next generation. This is one of the issues that has worried the Chinese leadership about the rising inequality observed since the end of the

1980s. To weaken this mechanism would require either taxing income (and perhaps wealth) progressively, or taxing inheritance.

The preceding overview shows us that the relationship between redistribution and economic efficiency is complex, multifaceted, and multidirectional, and that we must, in this area as in many others, guard against easy oversimplifications. Outside of its societal costs, excessive inequality of economic opportunities and results can have significant negative impacts on the volume of economic activity and the material well-being of society as a whole. Redistribution could therefore help us improve the functioning of the economy. But as it can itself be costly, its ultimate effect will essentially depend on the form that it takes and the significance, as well as the nature, of the inequalities that it helps to correct.

CHAPTER 5

Which Policies for a Fairer Globalization?

Building on the issues addressed in the previous chapter and their implications for the way in which inequality might develop in both the global economy and national economies, it is now time to return to the question we started with. Inequality is exploding within a large number of countries, with the potential negative consequences that we have just analyzed and, at the same time, standards of living in the world as a whole are converging. How can we maintain the trend toward increased global equality while curbing the rise in national inequalities that will, eventually, come into conflict with this first objective?

If the question itself is simple, the answer is anything but, primarily because it involves the interplay between the global economy as a whole and individual national economies, particularly those of rich countries. For example, if we believe that the increase in national inequalities is due above all to the globalization of trade, it would be tempting to try to remedy it by taking protectionist measures. Several figures in France and elsewhere in the world have come out in favor of this policy. Some have even advocated a policy of "de-globalization."[1] The problem is that even if such a policy did lead to a reduction in inequalities in some countries—which, as we will see later on, is itself doubtful—it would also be a hindrance to the development of other countries and would ultimately slow down the reduction of poverty in the world. This is exactly the kind of trade-off that a community that cares about global well-being must avoid. It is therefore important that we explore those policies that would allow us to pursue these two objectives simultaneously or in parallel. I will begin with policies at the global level and then look at policies aimed at correcting national inequality.

Policies toward a Global Convergence of Standards of Living and the Reduction of Poverty

As we have seen, it is likely that the convergence between emerging economies and rich economies will continue in the years to come, and perhaps even accelerate. Things are not so clear for poor countries, most of which are located in Africa, whose current development is based on exporting raw materials. A large number of these countries have experienced a period of growth since the early 2000s, largely thanks to high commodity prices on the world markets. But it is unlikely that this situation can be sustained over the long term. For global poverty to continue to fall,

[1] Jacques Sapir, *La démondialisation* (Paris: Le Seuil, 2011).

growth in these countries must remain high over the coming decades. Of course, growth is the responsibility of the
countries themselves, but, in poor countries, it is heavily
influenced by the international economic climate. As experience has shown us, it is difficult to intervene and control
prices on global commodity markets; we must therefore
look at the question of the support that the international
community, and especially the rich countries—but also, increasingly, emerging countries—can and should offer to
poor countries for their development.

Development Aid

Currently, development aid is the only true instrument of
international redistribution from rich to poor countries,
but its size remains quite limited and its effectiveness in
reaching those who need it most in poor countries is open
to debate.

Rich countries allocate about 0.35% of their Gross
National Incomes, around $130 billion in total, to devel-
opment aid, or *official development assistance*, as it is of-
ficially called, to poor countries. In comparison to the redistribution that takes place within nations, such sums
appear almost negligible. For example, the French system
of taxes and transfers redistributes around 15% of the income of the richest 20% (which is approximately the same
proportion as the population of rich countries represents
in the world) to the rest of the population. This is forty-five
times more redistribution than what we see at the global
level! For the countries on the receiving end, the sums of
money redistributed by development aid are nonetheless
far from trivial. In certain cases, development aid can ac-

count for up to 15% of national income, and sometimes more than half of the government budget.

Historically, the idea of official development assistance and the focus on reducing the income gap between rich countries and the Third World developed in the early 1960s, at the moment of decolonization. This humanitarian concern was clearly coupled with a geopolitical objective. In the midst of the Cold War, each side was trying to win the good graces of the countries in the middle, who often hesitated when it came to choosing which economic system to adopt, or which set of alliances to join. On the Western side, the International Development Association, a branch of the World Bank responsible for managing a large percentage of multilateral aid, and the Development Assistance Committee, which coordinates bilateral aid from OECD countries, were established. A few years later, the Pearson Commission would ask that rich countries commit to spending 0.7% of their Gross National Income on official development assistance.

This number was never reached. Some countries, notably the Scandinavian ones, kept their commitment, but they were too small to weigh heavily on the total numbers. From the end of the 1960s to the end of the 1980s, overall official development assistance stabilized at around 0.35% of the GNI of donor countries, or half of the stated objective. It dropped significantly with the end of the Cold War, proof of the important role geopolitics had initially played. It began to shift back upward again in the early 2000s, with the energetic mobilization of the United Nations in favor of the "Millennium Development Goals" with a target date of 2015. These goals include in particular cutting poverty in half, universal primary education, and the reduction of infant mortality rates by two-thirds.

This initiative, which is a concrete sign of the international community's will to fight to reduce inequality and poverty in the world, has returned the volume of development aid back to its earlier levels. Yet, it is not clear that the geopolitical or diplomatic motivation of aid has completely disappeared from the motivation of the donors. At the same time, new sources of funding have appeared that are not taken into account by the numbers given above. These include private organizations such as the Gates foundation, as well as emerging countries such as China, India, or Brazil. These sources of funding are growing. At present they represent a little more than 10% of the official aid from the developed countries, whereas they were close to negligible fifteen years ago.

What has been the impact of these monetary flows on development and the reduction of world poverty? Have they been effective in reducing poverty? For some time now, this question has been the subject of intense debates between partisans and critics of aid. For its partisans, only development aid can help countries emerge from the "poverty traps" in which they are often caught, given that on their own they are unable to finance the investments necessary for their economies to take off and for them to reach the millennium goals. Critics of international aid, for their part, emphasize the absence of any significant statistical correlation between aid and economic growth, and are skeptical that aid has truly contributed to improving the ability of recipients to bring people out of poverty.

Several reasons have been offered for this apparent failure. The primary explanation emphasizes governance, which is often deficient, and the levels of corruption observed in a number of recipient countries. As sovereign states are the recipients of official development assistance, the donors cannot really control the way that it is used without violating basic principles of national sovereignty. A large portion of aid therefore ends up being diverted, most often to the benefit of the leaders or their entourages. Everyone has heard of the immense personal fortunes that certain African leaders were able to accumulate, in part by embezzling development aid; between 1980 and 1990, Mobutu was able to amass a fortune of almost $5 billion in Zaire, and in just four years in the 1990s, Abacha managed to amass a fortune of $2–5 billion in Nigeria.

Actually, the issue of deficient governance in connection with aid is more serious than the mere diversion of aid flows by corrupt governments. Indeed, it might also be the case that development assistance itself bears some responsibility for bad governance by making the elite in recipient countries unaccountable with respect to their own population of the way aid is spent. From that point of view, aid has the same lack of transparency as the rent from natural resources accruing to governments. As such it could be said to help lock recipient countries into a cycle of bad governance and slow development—not only doing little to reduce poverty but actually contributing to the creation of more poverty by preventing appropriate institutional reforms and faster growth.

Should we therefore adopt the point of view of those critics of aid who urge poor countries as well as donors to turn down aid? Or, should we, as some researchers suggest, focus aid only on very time-limited projects and experiments to determine "what works and what doesn't" in development?[2] Alternatively, perhaps we should distribute

[2] See Dambisa Moyo, *Dead Aid* (New York: Farrar, Straus and Giroux, 2009) for the first approach; and William Easterly, *The White-Man's Burden* (New York: Penguin Books, 2006) or Abhijit Banerjee, "Making Aid

aid selectively, as is often the case today, by orienting it principally toward countries whose governance seems acceptable, and only to sectors where funds are supposed to be harder to divert, which is to say, social sectors such as health or education?

Without going to either extreme, I would suggest that there are a few simple principles that deserve to be taken into account. First of all, insofar as a large portion of aid has relieved poverty and improved the opportunities of the poorest individuals in the areas of health and education, it is hard to claim that aid is completely useless, even if it doesn't immediately boost growth. The observation and evaluation of projects funded by multilateral aid demonstrate that it has supported significant progress in these areas. Our fundamental concern should therefore be to ensure that aid is not diverted, that its volume is sufficiently high, in line with the commitments made by both donor and recipient countries, and that it is concentrated on poor countries.

We must then make a distinction between recipient countries whose leaders behave predatorily, even criminally, and those whose governments are more transparent or "development-oriented." Strict conditionalities and effective regulations must be imposed in the first case, even if this goes against certain principles of national sovereignty. Inversely, more transparent governments must be allowed to freely manage their development strategies and the usage of the funds that they receive, with aid being tied to results alone. Also, donors should require from recipient govern-

---

Work," *Boston Review*, July/August 2006, for the latter. A more recent strong critique of aid, which is also dismissing the experimentalist view of aid, is provided by Angus Deaton, *The Great Escape: Health, Wealth and the Origins of Inequality* (Princeton, NJ: Princeton University Press, 2013).

ments that they widely publicize the amounts being received, their intended use, and their actual use in the interests of clearer policymaking.

In donor countries, it also matters that the allocation of aid, its use, and its monitoring, are fully transparent to civil society. Such transparency might deter donor countries from allowing their own political interests and views about development to dominate their aid policies, as was the case during the Cold War, when geopolitical motivations influenced where aid was given, or subsequently with the structural adjustment policies imposed in the name of the Washington consensus upon recipient countries during the 1980s and 1990s. There also needs to be better coordination between donors to avoid replication of programs and to apply consistent management principles vis-à-vis the recipient countries. With this in mind, the ideal situation would probably be one in which the majority of international aid was managed by multilateral agencies free of preconceived notions regarding the best policies for economic development.

Other Channels of Redistribution between Rich Countries and Poor Countries

International aid is the only direct channel for redistribution between rich and poor countries. But there are also indirect modes of transfer, which do not always function in the same direction. In fact, any intervention that affects the economic flows between countries will modify, in some way, the international income distribution. This is true when it comes to trade, migrations, or movements of capital. Any restriction placed by a rich country on imports from poor countries will have a negative effect on standards of living in the latter. In the same way, the growing constraints imposed by developed countries on the immigration of unskilled labor has prevented potential migrants from developing countries from improving their well-being and/or those of their families through remittances. Another problem for poorer countries is that even when the banks in developed countries do grant them loans, which is not always the case, they will often demand excessive risk premia.

While important progress has been made in the liberalization of trade, this process remains incomplete. In particular, many poor countries have only limited access to the manufactured goods markets of developed countries. For several years now, the "Doha negotiations," first known as the "Doha Development Round," which are organized by the World Trade Organization, have been attempting to improve this situation. However, these negotiations have become bogged down and have effectively failed because they have focused almost exclusively on the relationships between developed countries and emerging economies (China, India, Brazil) rather than on those between rich and poor countries (principally raw material–exporting African countries), which are less strategically important in the current phase of globalization. Outside of raw materials, the access of poor countries to the markets of developed countries should be a priority, as should some coherent form of protection for their domestic markets. This is the only way these African countries will be able to diversify their economies, a necessary precondition for their future development and especially for their ability to absorb a rapidly growing labor force. Guaranteeing their access to the agribusiness and textile markets of developed countries could, in many cases, have a far more beneficial impact than aid.

One might think that these countries are not competitive enough to export anything besides minimally processed raw materials or agricultural products, and that they cannot truly compete with Asian or Latin American countries in manufactured or agribusiness products. It is true that they are often handicapped by a dramatic lack of transportation infrastructure, in terms of both roads and ports, and often by low levels of productivity which result from limited volumes of production. Aid for infrastructure construction and privileged access to developed markets through the temporary granting of trade preferences would allow these countries to overcome these handicaps, possibly with the assistance of foreign investors, including those from Asian countries.

Since the beginning of the 2000s, initiatives of this kind have been proposed by the United States (the African Growth Opportunity Act, AGOA) and by Europe (the Everything But Arms initiative, or EBA). The idea was that these programs would open American and European markets, duty- and quota-free, to African products under certain conditions: a limited number of products in the case of the AGOA (mainly textiles and shoemaking), and rules about the local content of exports, called "rules of origin," which turned out to be excessively strict, in the case of the EBA. The total impact of these programs was quite limited, but it is possible to imagine that their effectiveness might be improved. To this end, the recent initiative by a Chinese company (Huajian) to establish itself in Ethiopia to produce high-end shoes for export to Europe and the United States within the framework of these preferential trade agreements might be an advance sign that such a shift is taking place.

The Economic Partnership Agreements (EPAs) that the European Union is offering to regional unions of African countries generalize these trade preferences. In addition, they offer the advantage of incentivizing the creation of true customs unions and regional markets, which would expand the local outlets for African companies. However, they remain quite limiting when it comes to rules of origin and are far too exigent with regard to customs liberalization. In their current form, they risk being more of a handicap than an aid to the diversified development of African economies.

The restrictions that developed countries impose on trade with poor countries are not limited to the trade of goods. I mentioned migration earlier. I could have also mentioned intellectual property. We all remember the attempt by the pharmaceutical multinationals to sue South Africa, which had just passed a law that allowed for the production of generic AIDS medication. This dispute had a favorable outcome, as the multinationals finally dropped their suit. But the TRIPS (Agreement on Trade-Related Aspects of Intellectual Property Rights) accords remain in place, which in many instances restrict the access of poor countries to new technology and constrain their development.

The global redistribution that takes place through official development assistance is weak and fragile. A rough estimate suggests that, under the overly optimistic assumption that it were distributed equally among the inhabitants of recipient countries, it could contribute to a drop in the Gini coefficient for global standard of living of around 0.25 percentage points. This effect is minute in view of the figures seen in chapter 1, but it reflects the size of development aid relative to world income. It could be significantly complemented by policies of preferential trade coupled with infrastructure targeted aid that would facilitate the access of manufactured goods produced in poor countries to the markets of rich countries.[3]

One might think that policies such as trade preferences in favor of low-income countries and easing the migration of their population to advanced countries would be politically unacceptable in the latter. As far as trade is concerned, the issue is not so much with developed countries, as the production of the corresponding goods has already migrated toward emerging countries. Emerging countries would be those that would object to preferential trade regimes, unless of course they might gain from it by investing in poor countries, as in the case of the Huajian company. Things are more problematic with regard to migration, however, as this is a socially and politically sensitive issue. Yet, at some stage the developed economies will have to face up to their aging and declining population problem, for which immigration may be part of the solution.

There are therefore a wide range of policies that could accelerate the convergence of global standards of living while simultaneously making the world economy more efficient. As suggested in the preceding paragraph, there is also no reason why these efforts should be limited to the rich countries alone. When it comes to development aid,

---

[3] Protectionist barriers are still sufficiently strong today that it is uncertain whether the redistribution undertaken by rich countries to poor countries is to the net advantage of the latter. See François Bourguignon, Victoria Levin, and David Rosenblatt, "International Redistribution of Income," *World Development* 37, no. 1 (2009): 1–10.

trade preferences, capital, and labor flows, the emerging economies should be involved as well.

Correcting National Inequalities

Having recognized that the rise in national inequality, which is attributable in part to globalization, could harm economic efficiency (if only by provoking social tension that could potentially block essential economic mechanisms or adjustments), we must turn to the question of how to rectify these inequalities. There are several ways in which we could proceed, each one carrying its share of constraints and costs. The first involves current income, through taxes and transfers; the second focuses on the accumulation of productive assets; and the third focuses on primary income, through the modification of market mechanisms.

Redistribution through Taxation and Transfers

The most common method for correcting standard of living inequality is obviously taxation and, more precisely, the progressive taxation of income or uniform taxation of the revenues which fund transfers in purchasing power to the bottom end of the income distribution. Because rising inequality is often caused by the highest incomes, the first solution to rising inequality would seem to be simply raising the highest marginal tax rates on income, which would mean, in certain cases, returning to a truly progressive system of taxation. But things are not as simple as they might seem. There are political and economic limits on raising tax rates, and it is not clear that such a policy would correct for all of the aspects of rising inequality.

At present, the marginal tax rates on the highest income brackets are around 40–50% in the OECD countries. However, if we also include the mandatory deductions, or social contributions, on income from labor as well as indirect taxation on consumption, the rates in certain countries appear to leave little room for raising tax rates in a way that would not be incompatible with maintaining incentives. In France, the effective deduction from wages for each additional 100 euros in the top income bracket (already subject to the highest marginal income tax rate of 45%) is today between 60 and 75 euros, depending on whether or not we consider social contributions to wage income (particularly for retirement) as deferred income. Can we really go any further without significantly shrinking the tax base—either because of tax avoidance of varying degrees of legality, or because of a drop in the economic activity of these taxpayers—not to mention the risk that these individuals might leave the country altogether for a country with a lighter tax burden?

The preceding argument focuses primarily on income from labor. The tax rates on income from property are often quite a bit lower than the numbers mentioned above. What's more, since high incomes include a large proportion of income from capital, their effective tax rates are lower than they would be if the totality of their income was from salaries. Dividends and capital gains are taxed at rates of around 30% in OECD countries, resulting in a situation where the effective tax rate paid by the richest is often closer to this number than it is to the highest marginal tax rates on income. In the United States, the average tax rate on the richest 1% is only 35%. Billionaire Warren Buffett recently announced that he had been surprised to learn that he was paying, at the margin, a lower tax rate than his secretary. The effective tax rate on the richest 1% is about the same in France,[4] and thus a good deal lower than the highest marginal tax rates on income from labor. The same is true in a large number of developed countries.

Average tax rates of around 35% seem to leave some margin to raise taxes and decrease standard of living inequality. Given this, it is the tax rate on income from capital that should be raised. But the major obstacle to this—and one of the reasons for the asymmetry between the taxation of labor and capital—is the international mobility of capital, one of the core features of globalization. The worry is that raising the tax rate on income from capital would drive capital owners to invest it in other countries that have more favorable tax systems, as is notoriously the case with tax havens. In other words, there is a concern that tax evasion or optimization could shrink the tax base, resulting in a drop in tax revenue and in the volume of transfers to the lower end of the income distribution that these taxes make possible.

We do not have very precise estimates for the elasticity of the tax base in relation to the tax rate. It is therefore difficult to measure the room that states have to maneuver on this subject. A compilation of various studies by Emmanuel Saez, Joel Slemrod, and Seth Giertz provides a median esti-

---

[4] For the United States, see Thomas Piketty and Emmanuel Saez, "How Progressive Is the U.S. Federal Tax System?: A Historical and International Perspective," *Journal of Economic Perspectives* 21, no. 1 (2007): 1–24. For France, see Camille Landais, Thomas Piketty, and Emmanuel Saez, *Pour une révolution fiscale*. We should note, however, that in France's case, this number is modified by taking into account the *impôt de solidarité sur la fortune*, the solidarity tax on fortunes, or ISF. This figure ignores recent reforms on non-labor incomes launched by the Hollande administration and the temporary tax at 75% on earnings of more than 1 million euros imposed on companies paying such high salaries or equivalent.

mate of around 20% for the elasticity of top taxable incomes with respect to the marginal tax rates in the United States.[5] Given the tax rates observed there, this figure implies that when the government seeks to raise an additional dollar of tax revenue on top incomes, the behavioral response of taxpayers is such that the government would only get 72 cents. This estimate is only the middle of the range. At the top of the range of elasticity estimates, the net additional tax revenue would be around 55 cents.[6] Even though there are still smaller estimates in the economic literature, this is still quite a long way from zero, so it would seem that there would still be room in the United States for increasing taxes on high incomes in a way that would strengthen the correction of inequalities and increase tax revenues. It is also possible that these estimates rely on periods where the geographical mobility of the tax base was not what it is today. This should be checked carefully. As another example, the effective tax rate on income from capital has increased in France by around a third over the course of the last ten years and it appears that the tax base has changed very little.[7]

This being said, there must be a ceiling to tax rates, one that would most likely depend on the tax systems of other countries. The mobility of financial assets is real. Gabriel Zucman estimates that an average of 8% of household fi-

[5] See "The Elasticity of Taxable Income with Respect to Marginal Tax Rates: A Critical Review," *Journal of Economic Literature* 50, no. 1 (2012): 3–50.

[6] The 72 cents figure is taken from Emmanuel Saez, Joel Slemrod, and Seth Giertz, *The Elasticity of Taxable Income*, p. 9. The 55 cents figure is obtained by applying their calculation to the top of their range of estimates of the elasticity of taxable income.

[7] This was prior to the recent reforms by the Hollande administration aimed at closing the gap between the taxation of labor and capital income.

nancial wealth in developed countries is located in tax havens, with this number logically being substantially higher for high incomes and large fortunes.[8] Beyond a certain threshold of taxation, international coordination would become necessary if taxation is to be used to help correct for rising inequalities in rich countries. This is definitely a key issue.

Independent of short- and medium-term changes in the tax base, there is also the concern that, over the longer term, a rise in taxation might hinder a country's potential for innovation and creativity, and as a result its potential for growth. These are the kinds of distortions that were alluded to in chapter 4. It is difficult to estimate the elasticity of long-term aggregate economic performance with respect to marginal income tax rates. Nonetheless, we also know that the marginal tax rates in many OECD countries were significantly higher over the two or three decades after World War II than they are today and this does not seem to have been a major handicap to growth. In fact, the economies of most of these countries grew more rapidly at times when their tax systems were more progressive and their top marginal tax rates were higher. Of course, it is also true that other factors were at play and that the mobility of capital then was not what it is today. This fact should be understood in the context of the many studies that have attempted to find a correlation between economic growth and the average rate of taxation and generally end up with results that are not statistically significant.[9]

[8] Gabriel Zucman, "The Missing Wealth of Nations: Are Europe and the US Net Debtors or Net Creditors?" *Quarterly Journal of Economics* 128, no. 3 (2013): 1321–64.

[9] See in particular Peter H. Lindert, *Growing Public* (Cambridge: Cambridge University Press, 2004).

Even if the costs of a marginal tax increase do not seem excessive, the size of the increase that would be necessary to bring income inequality back down to where it was prior to the last two or three decades would be quite significant in certain cases, and the goal of returning to what we might call a "normal" level of inequality does not look entirely feasible from a political viewpoint.

The United States is the most extreme case of this. The share of household income after taxes and transfers going to the richest 1% doubled between 1979 and 2007. With an effective tax rate of 35%, a simple calculation shows that, at a first estimate, this rate would have to increase to 67.5% in order for the share of disposable household income going to the top 1% to return to its earlier levels,[10] which is quite a bit higher than the highest marginal income tax on the top bracket. A similar rate hike would be necessary for the United Kingdom to return to the levels of inequality that it saw in the 1960s and 1970s. But a reform of this size would be a revolution in a country that was unable to prevent the repeal of the increase in the highest marginal tax rate from 45% to 50%, which had been implemented at the beginning of the recent crisis! Taxation as an instrument might therefore not be sufficient to return inequality to its pre-increase levels in the countries that have experienced the largest rises in inequality. Either inequalities will remain high (although if any slightly ambitious tax reforms are undertaken, these levels might be lower than they are today), or other mechanisms for reducing inequalities will have to be found.

[10] This calculation goes as follows: by fixing the primary income of the richest 1% at 100, its disposable income is today 100—35 = 65. At first approximation, cutting this in half to return to the distribution of the 1970s would entail a total tax rate of 100—(65/2) or 67.5%.

For the time being, the situation is less catastrophic in the other OECD countries, either because their rise in inequality has been moderate, as in France, or because inequality itself remains low, as in Sweden. Increased redistribution through taxation remains conceivable in these countries, although of course within the limitations set by the international mobility of wealth and of its owners.

By focusing on the correction of inequalities through taxation on high incomes in developed countries, I have ignored the use of additional revenues. Of course, they can be distributed in a progressive way with a priority to low-income people. As a matter of fact, it is well known that in advanced countries the redistributive power of the tax-benefit system comes more from transfers to low-income people than from the taxation itself.

The risk of losing economic efficiency also exists with this form of redistribution, but it is of a different nature than what we saw with regard to high incomes. Here, it is specifically a question of the negative effects redistribution might have on the labor supply and the poverty traps that might be created by the mechanisms of social assistance. Guaranteeing a minimum income based solely on total resources falling below a certain threshold would not give recipients of this aid an incentive to find work, with the risk that they end up marginalized in relation to the rest of the population. Negative income taxes, such as the Earned Income Tax Credit in the United States, which are now fairly widespread across developed countries, manage to keep some of the incentives in place. There are similar kinds of questions about unemployment compensation and the implicit trade-offs this entails when it comes to the effort put into looking for work.

What I've written above primarily concerns developed economies. What then of emerging and developing economies, where inequalities are increasing or are already exceedingly high? The problem for these countries is, generally, that their systems of redistribution are not very developed, and that as a result the state's ability to reduce inequality through progressive taxation and transfers of income is very limited. For example, the weight of individual taxes on incomes as a percentage of GDP is 2.5% in China, 1.6% in Latin America, and 0.5% in India, while the average for OECD countries is around 9%. The main explanation given for this state of affairs is that observing income in emerging economies is difficult. Taxes on income are therefore deducted at source, which means that they essentially affect wages in the formal sector, in addition to leaving aside income from property. Today, however, both the middle and the upper class in emerging economies use debit or credit cards and have bank accounts that the government tax service could easily access. The argument for the unobservability of financial flows as a constraint on taxes has become increasingly weak, especially for better-off households. In the present day, it should be possible to significantly increase both the rates and the progressiveness of income taxes in emerging economies, which would give governments an instrument they could use to influence standard of living inequality. If this possibility is ignored, it can only be as a result of a sociopolitical balance that heavily favors economic elites.

Paradoxically, over the last decade, important progress has been made in a large number of emerging economies through the development of "conditional cash transfers" to the low end of the income ladder. These are money transfers granted to poor households on the condition that they educate their children or have them examined regularly by doctors. Starting with pilot programs such as the Progresa in Mexico or the Bolsa Familia in Brazil, these programs have now spread to a large number of emerging economies in Latin America and elsewhere. In China, the Di Bao is close to a minimum income program for urban centers. In India, an employment guarantee program serves a similar function for the rural sector. We have been able to observe that although they are relatively modest in size (1% of GDP or less) these various programs have had a tangible impact on the degree of inequality and poverty in these countries. The conditionality also seems to work. Several randomized impact evaluations were carried out in a number of countries taking advantage of the fact that some communities entered the program one or two years before the others. They generally show a significant impact on both the schooling and the health status of children. In Mexico, for instance, impact evaluation studies have shown that the Progresa program had increased schooling by more than 10% among the 12–17-year-olds and reduced ill health by 20% among children under age five. On the other hand, in both Brazil and Mexico, it is estimated that the conditional cash transfer programs reduced the Gini coefficient by one percentage point at a cost of less than 1% of GDP.

To come back to the overall levels of redistribution achieved in developing countries, it must be recognized that it is very much limited with respect to most advanced countries at both ends of the income spectrum. Benefits in kind and in cash transferred to the bottom are relatively smaller, whereas taxes charged on the top are much lighter. It is also often the case that some redistribution instruments work in a regressive way. In Brazil, for instance, the pay as you go pension system runs a large deficit because it pays pensions actuarially larger than past contributions to retirees who happen to be in the upper part of the income distribution. Through the indirect taxes that finance the deficit, the whole population pays for this extra income for well-to-do pensioners.

Redistribution via Educational Policies and Taxation on Wealth

Equalizing the distribution of income can be done ex post, as we have just seen, through taxation and transfers based on primary income. But it can also be done ex ante, by promoting equality of opportunity. As a practical matter, this means equalizing the distribution of factors of production held by agents that determine their primary income, which is to say principally human capital and physical capital (land, buildings) as well as financial wealth. As such, reducing the intergenerational transmission of wealth through adequate taxation should prevent the perpetuation of inequalities from one generation to the next. Similarly, leveling educational inequalities by standardizing the quality of schools and facilitating the access of the best students to higher education could, all else being equal, contribute to a less unequal distribution of income. What's more, and this is in line with my earlier analysis of ways that equality and economic efficiency can be complementary, progress made in the area of education may translate over time into faster growth.

This argument is just as applicable to emerging and developing economies, where we can also observe a significant correlation between inequality in levels of edu-

cation—generally measured by number of years of schooling—and inequality in standard of living. This correlation
is observed not only in cross-sectional studies that compare
countries at different stages of economic and educational
development, but also in the joint evolutions of the educational structure of the labor force and inequality within the
same country. For example, the reduction in inequality
that has taken place over the last few years in Brazil can be
explained in part by an increase in the proportion of the
labor force with secondary and tertiary education. The
same is true for several other Latin American countries as
well.[11]

Nonetheless, the effect that educational policies can
have on income distribution is not without ambiguities. It
is certainly true that making extended and higher quality
education more accessible to everyone is a good thing in
itself and undoubtedly contributes to the equalization of
opportunities in a society. But its effect on income distribution will depend on a number of factors. In particular,
even if these educational policies are able to benefit a large
number of people, one must also take into account the
medium-run development of the labor market and the demand for labor. Without some substantial economic
growth, individuals with higher levels of education will not
necessarily be able to find jobs and wages that correspond
to their new qualifications. In such a situation, the effect on
distribution will probably be quite limited, and the frustration caused will be considerable.

In developed countries, one can imagine that educational reforms might make it possible to lower the percent-

[11] See Nora Lustig and Luis Felipe López-Calva, eds., *Declining Inequality in Latin America: A Decade of Progress?* (Washington, DC: Brookings
Institution Press, 2010).

age of workers who are underqualified and underpaid. Such a policy might not have a tangible effect on the competition brought about by globalization, insofar as this competition, as we have seen, seems to be spreading toward mid-level skills. But it could potentially temper the rise in inequality that originates from the low end of the income distribution. Implementing significant reforms would require a careful examination of the quality of educational systems and of student cognitive outcomes. To this end, the results of the PISA survey of educational performance, which clearly demonstrate the relationship between student outcomes and students' social backgrounds, leave little doubt as to the importance of education in the fight against inequality. In 2009, the gap between the highest performing 10% of students and the lowest performing 10% was greater than 50% of the average score in the United States and the United Kingdom, as well as in Belgium, France, and Italy, and this gap has grown in several countries.[12] We can also observe that selection by standard of living in higher education has increased once again and in the United States, it appears to have overtaken ethnic or racial selection.

This evolution can be explained by the growing sums that privileged families are willing to spend on their children's education. Today this has even spread to preschool education, which we know is a determining factor in later academic performance, and, beyond that, in professional careers. According to Sean Reardon, the differences we see today in the academic performances of children from high- and low-income backgrounds are attributable in large part

[12] See the statistical tables in *PISA 2009 Results: Learning Trends, Changes in Student Performance since 2000*, Vol. 5 (Paris: OECD, 2009).

to these investments in preschooling.[13] An extreme example of investments of this kind is the wealthy New York
families that are prepared to pay astronomical sums to psy-
chologists who might be able to help their three- or four-
year-old child pass the entrance exam into highly selective
preschools, whose tuition fees can often be as high as
$25,000 per year. In fact, this extreme example is helpful
because it demonstrates the public interest served by creating a system of preschool education that is high-quality
and open to all, such as the one developed in Finland, a
country which, interestingly enough, happens to be at the
top of the PISA rankings, both in terms of the average
score and the lowest dispersion of that score.

A more direct method for transferring wealth to one's
descendants is through inheritance. Reducing inequality
ex ante can therefore be accomplished by taxing intergenerational transfers of wealth, as well as inter-vivos transfers
which are often advances on inheritances. Practices and
opinions about this vary. For some, this type of taxation is
triply inefficient. First of all, it amounts to taxing the same
income twice, first in the form of income taxes when the
beneficiary receives the income in his or her account, and
again when the wealth that this person has accumulated is
passed on to the next generation. What's more, it represents a clear disincentive against saving and investment, if
indeed one of the motivations of entrepreneurs and investors is the ability to pass on the fruits of their labor to

[13] See Sean Reardon, "The Widening Academic Achievement Gap be-
tween the Rich and the Poor: New Evidence and Possible Explanations," in
R. Murnane and G. Duncan, eds., *Whither Opportunity? Rising Inequality
and the Uncertain Life Chances of Low-Income Children* (New York: Russell
Sage Foundation Press, 2011). See also, from the same author, "The Great
Divide: No Rich Child Left Behind," *New York Times*, April 27, 2013.

their descendants. And finally, taxing inheritance threatens to cause businesses to leave the country, with negative consequences on growth, employment, and the government budget.

In the majority of developed countries, we observe a gradual reduction in the taxation of inheritance. In certain countries, it has been replaced with taxes on wealth and property, collected during their owner's lifetime, which, from a strictly economic perspective, is not all that different from taxing inheritance and would present the same inefficiencies. Other countries have simply abolished taxes on inheritance or wealth. This is the case with Sweden, for example, a country that is nonetheless renowned for its egalitarianism.

The arguments against taxing inheritance that are made in the name of economic efficiency or fortunes are not all convincing, in particular when the choice is to be made between taxing the transmission or the ownership of wealth, as is the case with taxes on corporate capital, personal wealth, or property. Taxing inheritance comes down to taxing wealth a single time at the moment of transmission, rather than once a year as would be the case with a tax on wealth. At any given point in time, the latter combines the wealth that an individual inherited from her parents with what she was able to accumulate from her own labor, entrepreneurial and risk-taking spirit, or patience. The dual objective of equality and economic efficiency would dictate that we should only tax the first of these two elements and leave the second one alone, but of course it is not possible to distinguish these two components of wealth at a given point in time. This is not an issue in the case of the inheritance tax, though a problem arises around the issue of the transmission of family businesses when only a descendant or relative might have the specific knowledge required to manage a company effectively, even if this is probably less likely to be the case with businesses larger than a certain size.

Another argument in favor of placing greater emphasis on taxing inheritance in developed countries, specifically in continental Europe, is that to the extent that the value of wealth is increasing relative to national income, the relative importance of inheritance is also growing. The intergenerational transmission of inequalities therefore threatens to play a larger and larger role in the formation of a generation's inequalities.[14]

If it were not for the question of geographic mobility of wealth and individuals, we would have good reasons for thinking that taxing inheritance would be a useful instrument for improving equality of opportunity. This would be even more true if the revenue from these taxes was used to fund initiatives that would improve the access of the lower classes to credit and the possibility that they themselves might accumulate wealth. That said, the constraints imposed by the possibility of moving to countries with less strict taxes on inheritance is certainly not something we can ignore, especially when it comes to large fortunes or family businesses. After all, in Sweden this tax, and later a tax on wealth, were both eliminated after two large family businesses, IKEA and Tetra Pak, emigrated due to the difficulty of intergenerational transmission.

Few emerging or developing economies have significant taxes on inheritance. For example, China, India, Argentina, and Mexico do not tax inheritance, even though the distribution of wealth is often far more unequal in these

[14] See Piketty, *Capital in the Twenty-First Century*.

countries than in many developed ones. Other countries, including Brazil, Chile, and Morocco, do tax inheritance, but the level of this taxation is quite limited. As with the taxation of income, we can nonetheless imagine that technological progress with respect to the tracking of financial flows and financial assets should facilitate the creation and collection of such a tax.

Reducing Inequality through Market Regulations

The last area in which public policy can affect income distribution is in relation to the functioning of markets and the manner in which this determines primary incomes. We saw in a previous chapter how the wave of market deregulations that began in the 1980s affected income distribution, and at times contributed to a rise in inequalities. Today, many of these markets have become quite competitive, and intervention in them is only considered justified to ensure that they remain competitive, or that security or environmental norms are properly respected. Yet, some strategic markets do not function transparently even though they have a huge influence on the economy as a whole as well as on the distribution of income. As we saw earlier in this book, this is true in particular for the financial and labor markets.

In the case of financial markets, there are two channels through which they can directly contribute to income inequality: a much higher scale of individual remuneration than in other sectors and the increased profitability of financial wealth above a certain affluence threshold. Intervening in either of these two channels through anything other than taxation is difficult. The ongoing international discussion about curbing discretionary remuneration, or bonuses, for bank executives and traders is evidence of this. Legislation controlling this has been voted in by the European Union, but we do not yet know whether it will be implemented by all partners or whether ways will be found to circumvent it. For instance, an important measure consists of limiting the proportion of bonuses in the total remuneration package to reduce risk-taking behavior. The big question is how to harmonize these rules with the big non-EU financial centers: New York, Geneva, Dubai, Hong Kong among them. If these rules are overly strict, regulation of remuneration risks encouraging the flight of individual talent and companies to more relaxed regimes. If they are not strict enough, these regulations risk being completely ineffective.

We may wonder what conditions do allow the financial sector to offer its executives such high levels of compensation, which end up spilling over into other sectors over time. From this perspective, it seems quite likely that the excessive remunerations offered by certain financial institutions are the result of the situational rents that they enjoy. In particular, returning to a strict separation between managing savings and offering loans to individuals or companies, and investing in financial markets,[15] would allow us to cease being held hostage to these giant banks whose risky investments threaten individual savings as well as the financing of the economy. It is in part this idea that some banks are "too big to fail" that has allowed them to extract the rents that make possible the astronomical remuneration they offer a portion of their employees. More gener-

---

[15] I.e., re-establishing some form of the Glass-Steagall Act in the United States, which was abolished in 1999.

ally, any regulation that would lower the probability of systemic risk and by extension decrease the pressure that the large financial institutions are able to exert on elected officials would have the same effect.

In the preceding chapter I analyzed the way in which regulating the labor market could affect the distribution of wages and incomes. In this area, minimum wage laws remain the primary instrument available to governments. These laws prevented a deterioration of the income distribution at the low end of the scale in France, at the cost, perhaps, of an increase in unemployment. In the case of the United States, it is difficult to ignore the link between the decrease in the real minimum wage during the 1980s and 1990s and the drop in the wages of the lower deciles of the distribution over that same period. Of course, if the minimum wage is set too high, it will have a negative effect on employment and will entail nontrivial social, economic, and budgetary costs. However, this can be avoided if the total cost of minimum wage labor is kept constant by reducing payroll costs, which in turn would be funded by increased taxation elsewhere. This was the kind of strategy that France and other European countries pursued in the 1990s. In sum, it amounts to subsidizing the employment of the lowest skilled workers in order to increase their wages.

Such measures may be a temporary response to some exogenous structural shocks hitting an economy. Yet, if the goal is to fight against poverty and inequality, it may well be that income transfer policies that help low-income families are more effective than a minimum wage legislation because they are less likely to distort the operation of markets. In the long run, however, human capital accumulation among low-wage workers would also be more efficient.

Must We Be Protectionists?

Let us take a look at another form of regulation that often comes up in public debates in developed countries, during these times of crisis: protectionism. Restricting the importation of certain products is seen as a way of protecting national producers from foreign competition, especially from countries with low labor costs. The argument is that reducing the level of competition will benefit domestic companies that specialize in unskilled or low-skilled labor-intensive production and raise the demand for domestic labor, which will reduce unemployment, increase the relative wages paid to this labor and, finally, lower inequality levels.

This line of reasoning is not incorrect. But we should be aware of the costs of this type of policies, beginning with an inevitable reduction in exports to the countries that are being protected against, a drop in the employment and remuneration in corresponding sectors, and the increase in the price of the protected goods. Taken as a whole, economic analysis suggests that the net benefits of such a policy would be negative.

But how significant is this cost? As strange as it may seem for such an important question, the answer economists give is rather vague. The reason for this is that it is impossible to experiment in this domain, so our evidence is based on theoretical models that simulate, according to certain hypotheses, how the economy might respond if certain barriers to international trade were either established or removed rather than being based on empirical data. Simple calculations for the world economy as a whole suggest that the profits lost due to tariffs amount to around 1% of GDP. Based on this, we could say that, inversely, doubling or tripling the existing barriers would cost only 1–2% of global GDP, and in fact could even benefit certain countries. This may not be a huge, one off cost to be paid for reducing inequality, athough probably much more than through more conventional methods like minimum wage or minimum income guarantees. Yet, the problem is that these projections under-estimate the true cost of these policies, because they don't take into account the dynamic gains of trade, that is, the gains in productivity that result from competition and trade, which are probably quite a bit higher than the static gains that would result from a superior allocation of productive activity. There is a similar degree of imprecision when it comes to estimating the impact that a greater degree of openness in international trade has on the growth of an economy.

In the current situation, we could nonetheless identify several serious obstacles to protectionist policies pursued in isolation by a country that seeks to prevent economic inequality as a result of greater globalization. First of all, if this protectionism is targeted at imports from emerging economies, it has to be multilateral. Otherwise, the same imports could simply pass through a country with lower tariffs (in the case of France, another member of the European Union). It is, moreover, unclear that all of the trading partners in a free trade zone would be able to agree on a list of products to protect.

Second, a proportion of the products imported from emerging economies are for mass consumption goods (clothing, shoes, toys, consumer electronics), which represent a large percentage of the consumption of the very same low-income households that these protectionist policies are intended to help. Their situation might improve in terms of wages and employment, but they would lose out heavily in terms of purchasing power and cost of living. It is not even clear that the net effect would be positive.

What's more, the idea of "imported products" and "exported products" can be misleading. In the present day, value chains are long and complex, which has introduced inextricable complementarities between domestic production and imports. The iPhone is a well-known example of this. The device brings together innovation and distribution value, which are primarily American developments, with a physical and electronic content that is produced in more than twenty countries, including many Asian, and assembled in China. "Protecting" against Asian production would in that case lead to rising prices for exports originating ultimately in developed countries.

Finally, when it comes to protectionism that targets Asian countries, the re-conquest of markets that have been abandoned by Western producers, such as clothing, toys, or kitchenware, would require such high tariff levels that domestic consumers would be heavily affected. Protections should therefore be focused on sectors where developed and emerging economies are still competing against each other, whether it be cars, pharmaceuticals, or aeronautics. But these are sectors in which developed countries still enjoy a sizable trade surplus. Thus, why protect and risk retaliation? It is also important to recognize that an economy's gains in productivity or competitiveness are in part tied to its import/export dynamics. A country protecting itself against international competition in a certain line of products would amount to closing itself off and forgoing the potential benefits of innovation in that line.

In sum, and on the basis of simple economic theory, we cannot a priori reject the hypothesis that a more protectionist approach to trade policy might help improve the relative income of lower skilled workers and reduce inequality in advanced countries. But such policies would have a huge cost and it is not even clear that, in absolute terms, those it intends to help would actually be better off. On top of this, today's global integration of the value chains has introduced a de facto complementarity between production activities in various parts of the world such that protectionism might in many cases have a self-inflicted cost.

The preceding arguments focus on developed countries, but the question of the role of protectionism is an important one for developing economies as well. In their situation, it is not clear that a quick and full liberalization of trade will always be the best development strategy. The infant industry argument, according to which temporary protections are necessary in order to encourage the development of certain activities, because they allow domestic producers to develop a market large enough to build up experience and be competitive at the international level, is certainly valid in the case of these economies, especially the poorest among them. Africa is a good example of this. As we saw before, it is unlikely that this continent could, over the long term, develop and absorb a rapidly growing labor force solely through the exportation of raw materials. The necessary diversification of African economies requires a period of industrialization that is currently incompatible with a fully open economy. On the other hand, this diversification might be feasible within the framework of regional customs unions that allow for expanded markets, while also temporarily protecting local businesses from Asian competition or, possibly, attracting foreign investment into the service of these expanded markets. Of course, a time frame would need to be set up for such a protectionist strategy, so as to avoid the development of inefficient rents in protected sectors and to ensure the credibility of such an undertaking. From this standpoint, the increasing ineffi- ciency of import substitution and the exhaustion of this strategy in Latin America in the 1980s were among the causes for the slow growth observed during this period.

What Do We Do Now?

What conclusions can we draw from this brief review of the damage that high and increasing inequality may cause to modern societies and the policy instruments available to curb or to stabilize its evolution?

In the first place, the negative consequences of excessive inequality cannot be over-emphasized. Those aspects of economic inequality that are due to unequal access to eco- nomic facilities, such as credit or a decent education, or to discrimination in markets for labor, goods, and services, and more generally to market failures, are responsible for inefficiencies of economic systems. Circumscribing them, even partly, could significantly increase total output and income in the economy. But economic inequality may also be socially, politically, and economically disruptive if it goes beyond some threshold, the level of which is not really known, and probably highly specific to each individual so- ciety. Under these conditions, it would be dangerous to let inequality keep increasing as it did over the last two or three decades in some countries.

In the second place, there are policies available to us which would keep inequality from increasing. Of special importance are those policies that allow for the correction of the market failures mentioned above, and which could simultaneously generate less economic inequality and more economic efficiency. There is still much to be done in most countries of the world, including advanced countries, in the field of education and job training, to make access or quality less unequal. Regulating more rigorously those markets that are partly responsible for the recent rise in inequality in advanced countries, financial markets in particular, is another option. Fighting all kinds of discrimination, whether based on gender, ethnicity, or even income, is a third one. How much can be achieved in that way is uncertain, but, even if it were only for educational policies, evidence is available that shows this would be far from negligible. One could object that as these policy options do not constitute a direct response to the forces behind the rise in inequality—globalization or technical progress—they do not address the root of the problem. But for a while at least they will help contain the symptoms.

Other tools are available to fight economic inequality on an ex-post basis, as opposed to the ex-ante policies discussed earlier. Taxes and transfers, including social protection, should definitely be used more intensively in emerging countries. They increasingly have the capacity for developing such fiscal instruments.

Such instruments do exist in developed countries, but there seems to be some resistance today to expanding them, even though in many cases it would simply be returning to a previous position. At the bottom end of the income scale, budgetary reasons are invoked for not expanding existing measures and often are used as an excuse to scale them down. At the middle of the income scale a hypersensitivity to possible tax increases has developed in many countries, with governments reluctant to consider creating new taxes or making the existing ones heavier. At the top end, finally, there is this view that, on the one hand, the international mobility of capital, income, corporations, and people, and, on the other hand, competitiveness requirements born out of globalization make it impossible to increase the overall progressivity of taxes. This resistance to more taxation may also be explained by political economy factors, not independent themselves from the recent evolution of inequality and the increasing influence of capital and the rich elite on governments' decisions.

To be sure, it is not clear whether we have enough knowledge about the various types of possible tax regimes and the constraints of globalization to evaluate some of the preceding arguments against further efforts in taxation. Yet, those constraints must be taken seriously. In particular, it is quite possible that the developed world is caught in a race toward the bottom in progressive taxation matters, each nation protecting itself against mobility by weakening its tax system. If this is the case, then only some form of international coordination may solve the problem. From that point of view, the recent initiatives by G20 countries to regulate the international activity of banks and the flow of capital to tax havens are encouraging. Recent initiatives by the United States to reduce tax evasion, the current negotiations between Switzerland, the United States, and some European countries to re-establish some transparency also go in the right direction. They could also be the sign that another kind of globalization is coming into being in the area of capital flows control.

At the global level, poor countries are the issue. If nothing is done, they may find themselves lagging permanently behind the advanced and emerging economies if the current cycle in commodity prices is reversed. It is clear that aid has to be maintained and at the same time reformed, but this will not be enough on its own. An engine of growth, different from commodities, has to be found. In view of the very fast population growth in these countries—two billion people in Africa by 2050—failure to do so would create a ticking time bomb.

A final question must be addressed: has inequality stabilized in the countries where it grew over the last few decades, or are there still forces pushing toward further increases? If the tools and policies we have discussed in this chapter can be implemented, and it is unclear today whether they can or will, they could reduce some of the current levels of inequality. It is obviously impossible, however, that new progressive reforms of tax and transfer systems could be introduced every time the pressure for more inequality increases. Moreover, because they do not necessarily address the causes of increasing inequality, ex-ante equalizing instruments will soon have a limited impact. It will then be necessary to think in more ambitious terms about how our economic systems work and the nature of the globalization process. But we are not there, yet.

CONCLUSION

Globalizing Equality?

Will the twenty-first century be remembered for the globalization of inequality? Are we headed toward a world in which the inequality that developed over two centuries *between* nations will gradually spread *within* these nations themselves? Will we witness a world in which inequality remains unchanged, but exists on our doorstep rather than 10,000 kilometers away?

This image of a hyperglobalized world, in which the disparities in standard of living within countries would reach the levels that we see today between inhabitants of different parts of the world, is fortunately not our present reality, and it is unlikely ever to be if we take action now. Of course, we have seen inequality increase in a majority of countries, notably in developed ones and drastically so in some cases. But, even in the countries where it is highest, such as the United States, the divide between it and the inequality we observe at the global level remains enormous. There is much less of a difference in standard of living between a rich American and a poor American, even though it is increasing, than between an average American and an average sub-Saharan African, who, as a matter of fact have been getting a bit closer to each other in the last fifteen years or so. Moreover, we have seen that while the globalization of trade and the mobility of labor and capital have a certain responsibility for the rise in inequalities within countries, they do not account for it completely. Through various domestic policies, the effectiveness of which unfortunately tends to shrink over time, countries may still influence the evolution of inequality within their borders and they should in theory be able to prevent it increasing to such a point that it becomes costly to the economy and to society.

At the global level, the good news is that inequality is decreasing thanks to a historically significant process in which the big emerging economies of Eastern Europe, Asia, and more recently South America and sub-Saharan Africa are catching up with the advanced economies. From this perspective, our only concern should be that the poor countries may not keep the pace of growth that has been observed over the last two decades due to the end of a favorable cycle in their terms of trade. For this reason, we should be heartened by the fact that the reduction of global inequality is at the moment an enduring primary international concern, as evidenced by intense mobilization around the continuation of the UN's Millennium Development Goals beyond their 2015 horizon. There are many things that will need to change politically in developed and emerging countries, as in the poor countries themselves, for both the millennium development goals and their post-2015 extensions to become a reality. The emergence of a global conscience, and one that is not tied strictly to the purely geopolitical calculations of the great powers, is an-

other way—and a highly positive one at that—that globalization and the fight against inequalities can work in tan-
dem. Practically speaking, however, past experience has
shown that this cooperation between poor, rich, and
emerging countries has to extend way beyond goal setting
and associated official development assistance for the lot of
those in poor countries to improve.

Under these conditions, global inequality should continue to decline for a long time. Then, all that it would take
to halt the globalization of inequality and preserve the positive side of globalization is for developed, emerging, and
developing countries to be able to control rising inequalities within their own economies. We have seen that, to
varying degrees, they have the ability to do so, but do they
have the will?

Emerging countries are in a unique situation. The rise in
national inequalities that they have experienced is often
tied to the mechanisms of economic development themselves and to the capacity of these countries, which is limited for the time being, to redistribute income, equalize
opportunities, and promote good governance. This capacity should increase with time and with further economic
development and it will be up to them to make use of it or
not. From this perspective, a powerful example is the reduction of inequality that took place in Brazil over the last
fifteen years, very much as the result of a number of ambitious domestic policies and even if it still has a long way to
go before inequality reaches the global average.

In developed countries, the instruments are already
available and redistribution is already sizable. The problem
is that globalization and international competition have
given these countries an incentive to reduce redistribution
and social protections in general, with the justification that

they must remain competitive and that these policies put a strain on the cost of labor. We can see this happening in many countries. This trend has been seen as largely independent of the process of globalization, but, actually, globalization is the main exogenous force that pushes everywhere toward an ever increasing competitiveness. Similarly, we must recognize that globalization is putting limits on the autonomy of any particular country with regard to taxation. A significant rise in the highest marginal tax rates on income or the equalization of the taxation of income from labor and income from capital carries the risk of causing some talent, capital, and businesses to flee to neighboring countries or tax havens.

Beyond this limited space in the field of taxation and transfers, political leaders who wish to halt the rise in inequalities may rely on policies aimed at more equality of opportunities within populations. As international competition again puts limits on regulating the intergenerational transmission of wealth through estate taxes, these policies should principally be aimed at leveling the playing field in education, job training, or retraining and health. This is certainly not a minor objective; on the contrary, it touches on the core issues of economic inequality and the way in which it is perceived in the public eye. Although an important goal per se, the problem is that the effects of these more structural policies will take time to manifest themselves and also that they are only an indirect response to the unequalizing effect of globalization. Over the short and medium term, taxation is the only effective means of correcting inequalities, but it is constrained by globalization itself.

The difficulty here comes less from competition with emerging countries than from competition with other developed countries. Given the deep transformations taking place in rich countries, in the midst of the deindustrialization brought on by emerging economies, each country is attempting to garner the maximum number of advantages to itself in the sphere of international competition. It is this competition that threatens to provoke a "race to the bottom" in terms of redistribution. It is out of concern for remaining competitive with respect to other developed countries that certain countries have tried to moderate wage increases and social protection, while encouraging entrepreneurship and innovation by cutting their tax rates relative to their neighbors.

Aside from the areas in which states still have some autonomy, the question arises as to whether the fight against inequalities should be a common undertaking, rather than the initiative of isolated countries. The argument that after a certain point inequality becomes inefficient, if only because it produces social tensions that can hinder economic activity, will come into play sooner or later. Is it possible to imagine that inequality will continue to increase in the United States and that half of the population will continue to be excluded from the distribution of the gains from economic growth? Is it possible to imagine that inequality in European countries could reach the levels observed elsewhere in the world? And yet this has been the trend over the last two decades and it is not clear that the recent crisis has changed this. Leaders tend to wait until the last minute to act. In this case, will the last minute be the moment when the negative effects of inequality explode, undermining social and economic stability? By then it will be too late to reverse this process.

Such a threat means we need a concerted international effort focused on redistributive policies and the fight against inequalities. Over the last three decades, there has been a kind of "contagion" of tax reforms among developed countries, which have tended to decrease the progressiveness of redistribution from high incomes. It is urgent that we tip the scales back in the other direction, but this time through a concerted effort at the international level. The recent initiatives that developed countries have undertaken to regulate the flow of international capital and the attractiveness of tax havens are encouraging in this respect.

In many countries, the political landscape seems favorable enough that such an initiative would not be rejected out of hand, and it is not unlikely that several emerging economies would follow suit. We are not yet at a point where one might recommend some kind of international taxation system that would be enforced in the same way by all countries in the world. This is clearly utopian for the time being. The goal at this stage would only be to make capital movements more transparent so that national governments retain some autonomous taxation power and thus some means to control the degree of inequality in their population.

In our contemporary world, avoiding the globalization of inequality and making the most of the full benefits of globalization requires national and international action of the type I have tried to outline herein, before more effective steps toward global policies promoting more equality between and within countries can be envisaged.

INDEX